Thackeray's Critics

THACKERAY'S CRITICS

An Annotated Bibliography
of British and American Criticism
1836-1901

by

DUDLEY FLAMM

The University of North Carolina Press
Chapel Hill

For
E. S. F.
and
M. E. H.

Acknowledgments

I wish to express my appreciation for the helpful assistance of the staffs of the New York Public Library, the Library of the British Museum, and the Columbia University Library, particularly Mr. Eugene P. Sheehy. To Professor Lionel Stevenson, I owe special thanks for his careful reading of the manuscript and his valuable suggestions for its improvement. I am grateful to the St. Olaf College President's Fund for a grant to aid in the publication of this volume. Finally, I am very indebted to Ellen Flamm for both aid and encouragement at all stages of the work.

DUDLEY FLAMM
St. Olaf College
Northfield, Minnesota

Contents

INTRODUCTION

Thackeray and the
Victorian Age

The importance of the criticism of Thackeray's work rests on the fact that he, as a writer, can be so wholly identified with the mainstream of English fiction in the nineteenth century. Thackeray's position is central in an age whose novelists sought the realistic mode in their works and whose readers looked to realism in fiction, above all else, as a measure of its viability. To be sure, fictional realism was a concept subject to change during the course of the century, but at no time was Thackeray's work thought to fall outside the pale of these formulations. During the latter part of the century new social theories as well as a new emphasis on certain fictional techniques account for attacks on his work, but none of these truly overthrew the ethos of realism which he had been instrumental in giving definition by the 1850's.

The most obvious reason for this continued acceptance is that Thackeray's work (his concept of realism itself) reflected basic similarities with the thinking of the age in spite of its satirical strain and its ability to provoke varied reactions. His fiction represented the life that the Victorians knew, or, more importantly, the life they were willing to know. The moralizing tenor, so evident in the work, and the circumspection shown in regard to certain Victorian pieties are but two of the traits that assured him his place as a true representative of the century. At the same time, however, he dared to come close to the limit of what might be said. It is not surprising, therefore, that the criticism of his work can often be regarded as an index of the self-criticism of the period.

1. *The Growth of a Classic Reputation*

The reputation that Thackeray made and held during the course of the nineteenth century at first grew only gradually. His introduction to a wide reading public came with the publication of *Vanity Fair* (1847-1848), after a ten-year period as a productive free-lance writer. Although he had to wait for fame, the works that were written during the earlier years not only strengthened his own hand, but provided readers with the chance to identify those strains in his work which were to predominate.

Thackeray's real career as a writer properly began in 1837 when he became a regular contributor to *Fraser's*. It was then that, as Gordon Ray says, "he achieved a distinctive style and point of view."[1] A result of this association was *The Yellowplush Correspondence*, serialized in *Fraser's* through 1838.[2] The last of the parts had hardly made its appearance when the Philadelphia publisher Carey and Hart issued its pirated edition of *Yellowplush*, which was, in fact, the first book-form presentation of Thackeray's literary work.[3] The occasion was an auspicious one, for it indicated that the firm, then the leading publisher of belles lettres in America, had singled out Thackeray's work just as it had Dickens' when it had published *Pickwick* the year before. Although *Yellowplush* presented Thackeray to American readers, it did not initiate a program for publishing all of his English periodical writing that was to follow in the next ten years. Between *Yellowplush* and *Vanity Fair,* therefore, the

1. Gordon N. Ray, *Thackeray* (New York, 1955, 1958), I, 226.
2. Publication dates for Thackeray's work can be found in Lewis Melville's [pseud. of Lewis S. Benjamin] bibliography, *William Makepeace Thackeray* (London, 1910), II; or for American publications, Frederick S. Dickson's bibliography in James G. Wilson, *Thackeray in the United States* (London, 1904), II.
3. *Flore et Zephyr* (London, 1836) consisted of only eight drawings without text.

only other books of his published in America were *Stubbs's Calendar* (Boston, 1842), *The Irish Sketch Book* (New York, 1844), *Notes of a Journey from Cornhill to Grand Cairo* (New York, 1846), and *Jeames's Diary* (New York, 1846). These did manage to keep Thackeray's name alive, though they hardly provided the fullest opportunity for Americans to assess his talents. In England the situation was different. Though the bulk of that which he was writing was not reviewed because it was published only in magazines, at least his work was reaching the reading public.

The English reviewers' recognition of Thackeray rightly began in 1840 with the book publication of *The Paris Sketch Book*. It was greeted enthusiastically, gathering comments that praised the writer's "thoughtful truth and fiery sarcasm" (No. 9),[4] and his "hostility to humbug" (No. 12). In view of the slightness of this work (six brief stories and eleven articles), it is interesting that the keynote remarks about it were essentially foreshadowings of criticism that was to be made about *Vanity Fair* itself. Another example of this was the *Times's* ability to call into play the doubtful critical distinction that realistic representation betrayed a lack of artistic creativity. Thackeray's descriptions were praised for following "closely to nature," but this suggested to the reviewer that Thackeray had "drawn less on his creative capacity than on his recollection" (No. 7). The essence of this criticism was to become in the fifties a cause of serious debate, especially in connection with the inevitable comparisons of Dickens and Thackeray. The nature of these remarks that *The Paris Sketch Book* occasioned thus raises the issue regarding the degree to which the earliest critiques of an author set standards that in turn restrict future criticism by suggesting what readers should look for in subsequent work. This is important in regard to Thackeray's later work (particularly *Esmond*), which often suffered inadequate interpretation because of such critical limitations. The focus created by this early and minor work, therefore, strongly suggests that the elements isolated for praise were

4. Numbers indicated in parentheses refer to entries in the bibliography.

to a large measure critical desiderata of the time that could be handily applied to Thackeray. Ideally, it would be useful to examine some criticism of the early forties about a longer and fully realized fictional work of Thackeray, in order to confirm the judgments occasioned by *The Sketch Book*. This, however, is not possible. Though *Barry Lyndon* provides the example of the fiction, because of its periodical publication (*Fraser's*, 1844) there were no reviews, and a sense of its impact on the public must be arrived at indirectly. When it was published in book form in 1856, Fitzjames Stephen was able to call it the "best executed of Thackeray's work." Its relative brevity (compared to *Pendennis* or *The Newcomes*) and its unity of tone recommended the book "artistically" (No. 375). These were views which Brander Matthews could endorse forty years later, also noting, as had Stephen, that it was a book "shamefully neglected" (No. 643). One explanation that may account for the neglect of the book can be found in one of Thackeray's critics less concerned with the "artistic" excellence of a work and more devoted to assessing the view of life presented. Theodore Martin found cause to reject "pictures of tainted humanity," and he believed that "there are many things in life which it is better not to know" (No. 258). That *Barry Lyndon* was a prolonged exercise in irony was not much of a saving grace. Seemingly, many readers had little taste for irony and preferred to feel offended by the kind of life that in fact was represented. They seemed to prefer gentle satire directed at subjects hardly calling for strong feelings of indignation. Even *The Paris Sketch Book* had been able to incite one reviewer to say that its satirical humor was "too severe and biting to be pleasant" (No. 8). Although this insistence on a certain propriety of tone as well as substance was to be modified in the criticism of work after *Vanity Fair*, it nevertheless remained a critical dogma in Thackeray's lifetime. An examination of his work is bound to suggest that to the degree that Thackeray abandoned a youthful sense of disillusion or bitterness (or at any rate tempered this feeling when incorporating it into his fiction), his work grew closer to the optimistic view of human nature that the age wanted to hold. Even a critic like George Lewes, in so many respects above the platitudes of his time, gave support to this view. When reviewing *Esmond* he was able to declare it "a beautiful book" because "the mocking spirit has fled" (No. 199).

Part of the disfavor towards irony or satire in fiction seems to have rested on the readers' doubts that the work might indeed be an instance of a negative exemplum, something to be shunned. Apparently this problem did not exist for a work of non-fiction, and this may account for the great success of *The Snobs of England*, which increased the circulation of *Punch*, the magazine in which it was first published in 1846.[5] When this work did appear as a book (England, 1848; America, 1852), notices of it were able to identify its relevance to *Vanity Fair* and to Thackeray's fundamental social criticism. (See, for example, Nos. 68, 191, 193.) Though it could not placate readers who found his satire harsh, it could at least clarify his intention as a satirist, unmistakably pointing out one of his prime targets for attack. To a great extent, therefore, the anatomy of snobbery prepared the English public for *Vanity Fair*.

Vanity Fair was published in monthly parts in England from January, 1847 to July, 1848. With only the sixth number out, one reviewer felt justified in declaring that Thackeray's fame was assured for all time, that he had proved himself "the Fielding of the Nineteenth century" (No. 55), an epithet that was to become a commonplace in Thackeray criticism. Equivalent praise followed in succeeding reviews that found the uniqueness of the work in its realism. It provided "a literal photograph of the manners and habits of the 19th century," a history of "average sufferings" (No. 91). But it also transcended a mere depiction of external details and developed characters of truly human complexity (No. 70). In America, after the Harper edition appeared in August, 1848, critical comments noted the same qualities. Edwin Whipple cited *Vanity Fair* as "an attempt to

5. M. H. Spielmann, *The History of Punch* (New York, 1895), p. 318.

represent the world as it is," in contrast to the distortions that so many other novelists were providing (No. 82).

The insistence of these critical comments on the novel's realism suggests that this was a quality wholly new. Any such implication must be modified, since realism was indeed an ingredient in English fiction long before Thackeray. Further analysis of the responses indicates that what Thackeray did was to bring the realist's methods to bear on a part of life that had been previously treated in a different way—as romance, in the main. It was as a contrast to the novels of society that preceded it that *Vanity Fair* made so great an impact in England. In the United States a similar contrast, but with the full range of popular romances rather than with those dealing only with society, seems to have been at the core of the public's approval. Ever since the days of Scott, the pirated editions of English books in America were largely romances, and the works of native American writers also followed that mode. It was this antithesis that prompted George Strong, a New York lawyer, while praising Thackeray's realism, to add: "The elements of what we called Romance are but a cheap substitute, after all, for the awful interest of everyday realities."[6]

The realism alone of the work, however, would not have assured the success of *Vanity Fair*. Even among critics who thought highly of the book, there were any number who again raised the issue that it showed a preference towards the depiction of the meaner aspects of life, as had so much of Thackeray's earlier work, but that his purpose for presenting this aspect redeemed it. His satire and irony were here being used to point up moral truths (Nos. 69, 73). Charles Bristed went so far as to declare Thackeray "greater as a moralist than as a humorist," and *Vanity Fair* "a book to keep and read" because "there are many sermons in it" (No. 78). This view of him was not so far from the one he took of his own role. Writing to Mark Lemon of *Punch* in February, 1847, Thackeray included himself among

6. *Diary of George Templeton Strong*, ed. Allan Nevins and Milton Thomas (New York. 1952), I, 330.

those "who set up as Satirical-Moralists" and have "such a vast multitude of readers whom we not only amuse but teach."[7] The qualities of realism and didacticism therefore complemented each other. Critics often seemed to be saying that the best or most forceful example of a moral truth was one that the occurrences of everyday life confirmed. Thackeray's work, by partially fulfilling this standard, helped to raise the prestige of the novel as a form in the eyes of his contemporaries. In place of the notion of it as a fiction—a lie—embroidered by wish-fulfilling fancies, the realistic morality which readers found in his work bespoke its utility as a means of instruction—something much more in keeping with the moral earnestness that mid-nineteenth-century Englishmen and Americans were seeking.

Whereas the demand for didactic content served to promote the novel without causing readers seriously to misconstrue the fiction, in other ways the expectancies of readers created limitations that circumscribed criticism. One example of this was in regard to the low-key ending of the novel. Though critics mentioned the tone of disillusion in *Vanity Fair* and its lack of a conventional plot, neither in England nor America was the fact explicitly discussed that no character in the book enjoyed a completely successful outcome of his affairs. It is worth noting this inability to read the novel as a story with an unhappy ending, if only because Thackeray himself was set on writing that kind of story. In a letter to Robert Bell, the critic of *Fraser's*, Thackeray explained that Amelia was especially made to be "a silly little thing" in order to make clear that Dobbin was a fool for marrying her. He went on to add: "I want to leave everybody dissatisfied and unhappy at the end of the story—we ought all to be with our own and all other stories."[8] The critics of *Vanity Fair* did not explore this phenomenon, and in the face of the subtitle, "A Novel Without a Hero," they sought heroes and heroines of the customary variety and tried to grant them some measure

7. *Letters and Private Papers*, ed. Gordon N. Ray (Cambridge, Mass., 1945-1946), II, 282.
8. *Letters*, II, 423.

of success. If they did in fact sense Thackeray's true intentions, they skirted any head-on engagement with such ideas because of their uncharted dangers, and in no way was the book's popularity impaired on this account.

Vanity Fair made Thackeray a valuable property for both British and American publishers, and it set him up as a real challenger to the popularity of Dickens. While the monthly numbers of *Pendennis* were coming out (1849-1850), Dickens began to issue *David Copperfield*, and the contest between the yellow and green wrappers became the focus for intensive comparison. The relation between the two writers had many aspects which their contemporaries tried to explore, and these two books, because similar in certain respects, permitted the full range of differences in their styles to be enumerated and scrutinized both in England and America (e.g., Nos. 134, 147, 148, 149). One of the principle points of critical focus that such comparisons returned to was the seeming discrepancy between a writer's powers of imagination and realistic representation. David Masson, in an article that labored to do equal justice to each writer, tried to clarify this issue by alluding to the "real" and "ideal" schools of painting, in which the former copied the scene with an exact ("photographic") likeness and the latter "idealized" it. But despite Masson's attempted objectivity (and even a very slight preference for Thackeray), he was forced to conclude that the "real" was indeed less imaginative than the "ideal" (No. 148). Though there was consensus in this view, it does not seem to have hindered the reception of Thackeray's work.

More pertinent in regard to Thackeray's popular reputation was the feeling about *Pendennis* that was expressed in the rhetorical question: "Why must Mr. Thackeray be always 'going to the fair'?" (No. 131). Not only does this comment suggest that the book was overshadowed by *Vanity Fair*, but also that there were growing misgivings about Thackeray's disheartening view of human nature. Nevertheless, the novel immediately claimed staunch enthusiasts, such as George Lewes who thought it had a "generous view of humanity" (No. 134), and William Dean Howells who, in retrospect, believed it to be Thackeray's "greatest book" (No. 626, p. 131); and in years to come *Pendennis* would be appraised in its own terms and for its own particular merits (e.g., No. 700).

In the preface to *Pendennis* Thackeray wrote what might seem his own indictment of Victorian prudery. "Since the author of *Tom Jones* was buried," he wrote, "no writer of fiction among us has been permitted to depict to his utmost power a MAN. We must drape him and give him a certain conventional simper. Society will not tolerate the Natural in our Art." However, because Pen's love affair with Fanny Bolton is itself treated with the greatest possible circumspection (avoiding the slightest suggestion that anything improper occurs), Thackeray's prefatory statement becomes more of an apology for the fiction that follows. And though he may be criticized for a want of boldness, the justness of his practice in terms of his contemporary readers is only too apparent. *Fraser's* praised his restraint in not "drawing a MAN" on the theory that no book should be written that a father could not permit his daughter to read (No. 139). Clearly, Thackeray was well aware of the strictures that his age placed upon fictional realism and to some extent he tried to keep in mind the admonitions of his critics. But he also tried, by suggestion and innuendo, to come as close to the borderline of propriety as he could, and time and again his work provoked criticism about the substance of its reality, rather than analysis in regard to the novelist's skills of presentation. The response to *Esmond* provides an example of this critical bias and its attendant limitations.

Esmond was published in the fall of 1852 both in England and America. It was a book upon which Thackeray had labored greatly—the only one of his major novels which he finished completely before publication and which was not first presented in monthly parts. Its artistry was recognized by many at the same time that its story was found offensive. More widely and completely reviewed than *Pendennis*, *Esmond* tended to strengthen Thackeray's reputation as an artist, though its popular success was more limited than any other major novel. There was also an undercurrent of critical opinion, however, which tended to reduce the novel's virtuosity of style and descriptions of a past age to something of a sterile tour de force. When this attitude is examined in the light of the outright hostility to the essential substance of the story, it seems to suggest that it was a criticism adopted as the most obvious safe alternative—one that permitted reluctant praise. Thus the negative responses aroused by the central love story are an indication of Thackeray's ability to stir the public, and the reviews of *Esmond* become interesting as indices of popular sentiment and critical limitation.

Esmond was a departure from Thackeray's previous work in that it was a chronicle of one family, in which the characters were most readily understood in terms of their individual psychologies. Taine, the French critic, whose requirement for a novelist was that he be a psychologist, representing character without blame or mutilation, thought *Esmond* was Thackeray's only novel because the point of view towards the characters and events of the story distinguished it so markedly from his other major work.[9] English and American reviewers did not fully observe this qualitative difference.[10] Instead of looking for the uniqueness of *Esmond*, they sought out similarities to *Vanity Fair*, *Pendennis*, and even lesser works, and they missed much of the novel's interest.

The main quality that commended the novel to American critics was its historical aspect—its re-creation of the age of Queen Anne (Nos. 210, 218, 257). Though a limiting view, this ultimately did less injustice to the work than the approach of the English critics who looked upon the book as a sample of that variety of novel predominating in the 1850's—the domestic

9. Hippolyte Taine, "William Thackeray," *Revue de deux mondes*, VII (Jan. 1, 1857), 188.
10. Only George Brimley's review (No. 201) began to indicate the importance of Lady Castlewood and the fact that the entire story was the record of Esmond's attachment to her.

novel. This focus on the family affairs of the Castlewoods and the love triangle of Esmond, Beatrix, and Lady Castlewood led these critics to regard the ménage as not only disreputable but depraved. Esmond's marriage to Lady Castlewood was thought of as incestuous. In a scathing review, which cut short the possibility of the book's popular sale in England,[11] Samuel Phillips pronounced his final impression of *Esmond* to be "one of unaffected disgust" because the hero married his own "dear Mother!" (No. 221).[12] The attack once made prompted others to repeat it (Nos. 251, 258, 311), and eventually influenced American criticism to follow the same line of objection. The remarks ran the gamut from trivial discontent to wholesale condemnation of Thackeray's ideas about life. On the slightly ludicrous side are the reviewers who discussed the marriage merely in terms of the most superficial of their own personal preferences. While one writer could say that an older woman was hardly a desirable wife for an ambitious young man (No. 253), another could declare with equal aplomb that "the 'Marrying Man' will at once agree in the wisdom of his [Esmond's] choice" (No. 217). More strenuous objections complained that Lady Castlewood's ability to mourn her husband and harbor a love for Esmond contradicted all experience (No. 212); she (at forty) was long past the age for love or marriage (No. 251); and Esmond could hardly be thought admirable for loving a daughter and her mother at the same time (No. 266).

Once the critics had taken up the cudgels of defending the marriage mores of the time, any chance for legitimate analysis was lost. Nor was this tendency to brand the delicate love relationship a "perversion which sickens the heart" (No. 357) a quickly passing thought. It persisted (though with lesser acerbity), finding expression as late as 1900 when Howells referred to the marriage as an "unhandsome dénouement" (No. 698).

11. *Letters*, IV, 125.
12. The facts of the matter are that Esmond came to live with the Castlewoods when he was twelve years old and Lady Castlewood, then twenty, cared for him as a mother until he reached manhood. The marriage took place when she was forty and he was thirty-two.

By the early fifties, following the success of *Pendennis*, Thackeray's prestige was high and this climate of renown was conducive to the public lectures which he undertook in England in 1851-1852 and in the United States in 1852-1853. The lectures on the English humorists of the eighteenth century, an outgrowth of his researches for *Esmond*, succeeded mainly because he was thought to be just such a humorist as the men he discussed (No. 156). Notwithstanding his black-and-white portrayal of Swift, for which several of the notices rebuked him, his moralizing on the personal foibles of the great writers was close to the hearts of his listeners. In America the lectures served the additional function of enabling the general public to meet the man and to construe his personality with more accuracy than thumbnail biographical sketches had permitted. From these (e.g., No. 107) and from his reputation as the satirical author of *Vanity Fair*, an image of a rakish young fellow had developed. Thackeray's sedate and kindly appearance overthrew this notion. The American trip also gave Thackeray the opportunity to conclude agreements with American publishers to receive payment for his work, so much of which had been merely pirated before. Thackeray reckoned that his visit to America would have been worthwhile for these agreements alone, which would add about forty per cent to his future royalties.[13]

Another series of lectures, those on the Georges of England, were delivered in America in 1855-1856, after the publication of *The Newcomes* when Thackeray's repute was its greatest. But despite the public's favorable predisposition, these lectures were received with less acclaim than the *Humourists*, though they did serve Thackeray's purpose of making a great deal of money.[14] The charge that he was pandering to democratic sentiments by anatomizing four kings of England was levelled at him from both sides of the Atlantic (See Nos. 333, 358). In addition, the tone of some of the criticism in the American press rankled Thackeray (e.g., Nos. 334, 343), and led him to declare on the eve

13. *Letters*, III, 158.
14. Ray, II, 263.

of departure: "I fear I'm not near so good an American as I was after the first visit."[15] The *Georges*, however, were better received critically in Great Britain (1856-1857), perhaps because the subject was more familiar to the listeners, and perhaps, too, because they afforded a certain implicit comparison of the improprieties of certain Georges with the tranquil domesticity of Victoria. In this sense the author once again confirmed himself the true contemporary of his admiring public.

The work that had raised Thackeray's popularity to its highest level in the fifties and which marked the true peak of his critical acclaim was *The Newcomes* (1853-1855). It was a book that suited Victorians in almost all respects. Not only was it the sort of panoramic novel that readers expected from Thackeray, but it also suggested a mellowing of the author. It was thought of as Thackeray's masterpiece, presenting "life under its ordinary aspects" (No. 321), and demonstrating "with how deep a sympathy he can approach all that is good" (No. 319). Though the novel permitted Thackeray to exercise his role as "week-day preacher" and to strutinize weakness and vice, it also provided "gushes of tenderer feelings, gleams of heavenlier light, a deeper pity and a more tearful love" (No. 320). The oft-recurring charge that so much of Thackeray's work was expressive of cynicism and a narrow view of human nature, though it would never disappear completely, nevertheless became, after *The Newcomes*, less serious and less frequent.

Particularly responsible for permitting the book to create this heart-warming impression was the characterization of Colonel Newcome, and especially the pathetic death scene. Assuredly this struck the right note for contemporary readers. Hawthorne had this to say about it. "I read all the preceeding [*sic*] numbers of *The Newcomes* to my wife, but happened not to have an opportunity to read the last, and was glad of it— knowing that my eyes would fill, and my voice quiver."[16] Though

15. *Letters*, III, 608.
16. *The English Notebooks*, ed. Randall Stewart (New York, 1941), p. 225.

present-day opinion may consider the sentiment surrounding the Colonel's death as over-ripe, most nineteenth-century readers did not believe so. As late as 1897 it was possible for an article to cite this scene as an example of Thackeray's restraint in rendering the pathetic (No. 645).

The sentiment and realism that so appealed to readers of *The Newcomes* was indeed nothing new, and the fact is that even more ambitious critics found themselves hard-pressed to find terms of praise or analysis uniquely applicable to this novel. Essentially they relied on the standards that had been used to judge *Vanity Fair* and *Pendennis*. As had these earlier works, *The Newcomes* served as an ideal focus for discussing the presumed opposition of realism ("photographic" representation) to creative imagination, and the novel of "men" (character) to the novel of "manners." It likewise called into question theories of plot and dramatic unity. The majority of critics, it may be said, resolved these matters in a way favorable to Thackeray, and *The Newcomes* was considered the book that best exhibited the maturity and range of his talents. Year after year its "epic" quality continued to give it a place of central importance among his works (e.g., No. 677); in the nineties it was second only to *Vanity Fair* in popularity.

The fiction that appeared in the succeeding years did little to enhance Thackeray's reputation. In varying degrees *The Virginians* (1857-1859), *Lovel* (1860), and *The Adventures of Philip* (1861-1862) elicited the charge that his powers were waning, that he was becoming repetitious and wearisome. About any of these novels it could always be said, as it was of *Philip*, that "nothing that a good writer produces is positively bad" (No. 443), and indeed readers were able to find something good in each of the books. There was a willingness to accept Thackeray's work and to hope for something better each time. As Henry James said many years later, recalling the posthumous publication of the unfinished *Denis Duval*: "There was such a thrill, in those days, even after *Lovel* and *The Adventures of Philip*, at any new Thackeray" (No. 702).

Though *The Virginians* was better received than the books that followed it, the scant praise of it—primarily as a sample of historical fiction—was tempered by a widespread belief that it badly lacked artistic organization, especially any balance between the stories of the two brothers. The notion that Thackeray had tried to include too much may have partially explained this failure but it did not excuse it (No. 410). In the United States, notwithstanding the generally congenial attitude towards historical fiction, the American scenes of the novel ran afoul of criticism concerning the accuracy of historical and geographical detail. But by far the most serious complaint there had to do with Thackeray's attempt to portray George Washington as a human being, a depiction that was considered by many to be an insult to the myth of the national hero (Nos. 413, 420). Yet, in the face of all this displeasure with the novel, it earned more money for Thackeray than any other single work.[17]

In contrast, *Lovel* appeared and disappeared with little notice of any sort. It was more scantily reviewed than some of the earliest work that had preceded *Vanity Fair*. The singular virulent attack on it, proclaiming that its "ingrained vulgarity" left the reader with a sense of "moral deterioration," seems wide of the mark and suggests extra-literary reasons for the article (No. 427).[18] More plausibly, it was the very thinness of *Lovel* that was most disappointing to a public used to more substantial work from Thackeray.

Slightness, however, was not the defect of *Philip*. In spite of Thackeray's full efforts to present a vital full-length portrait of a young man, as he had done in *Pendennis*, *Philip* merely made the critics think that Thackeray was playing the same tune though with less skill (Nos. 438, 441, 444). The novel was essentially considered a "second-hand performance" (No. 443), and it is difficult not to see the justice in the adverse criticism,

17. *Letters*, IV, 155.
18. See Ray, II, 405.

because in many ways *Philip* does reflect carelessness. Nor in terms of Thackeray's own standards of realism would it be easy to defend the wondrous appearance of the lost will in the sword-case which sets all matters right in the end. None of these later works were to be regarded in future years as representative of Thackeray's true capacity, and they therefore played an even smaller role in his posthumous appraisal than they did during his lifetime.

The qualities that at all recommended Thackeray's last works —besides the mere momentum of his popularity—were his ability to provide characters with whom the public could establish a kind of personal rapport as if they were living acquaintances, and his continued assumption of the role of satirist-moralist, or lay-preacher. Assuredly, many readers found his moralizing tendency, his digressions and asides, an infringement on the novel form, but many more did not. In reply to the charge that such preaching stopped the story of *The Virginians*, Hepworth Dixon could answer, "Who cares? . . . The test of a good story is that it can be stopped without harm!" Moreover, "most of these sermons are delightful for their insight and their satire" (No. 402). This view was given strong confirmation by the American critic George Curtis. Reviewing *Philip*, he wrote: "You may sneer at this eternal lay-moralizing, but there is more meat in the nut he offers us than in many of a stronger and spicier flavor. His books are to return to. They are not read for the plot, but for the portraits" (No. 440). Another writer, considering Dickens and Thackeray in 1860, believed that the productions of both men were beginning to show a decline. Thackeray, however, seemed to fare better by comparison, primarily because he was a "better moralist, a more trustworthy teacher" (No. 423). These, then, were the grounds that permitted a spirit of acceptance, though not one of full-voiced praise, to prevail during the last years before Thackeray's death in December, 1863.

The obituaries and eulogies that appeared following his death were, as might well be expected, glowing tributes to him as a writer and as a man. The past prejudices of critics as well as some of their sterner judgments of his work were set aside in place of praise for what indeed had been his accomplishment. Most important was the sense of shared pride of achievement that informed many of the articles. The *Reader*, for example, could say: "Thackeray was characteristically a Victorian—pre-eminently a writer whom our era can claim as, both chronologically and by the cast of his genius, belonging to itself" (No. 457). Nor were such sentiments and the accompanying recognition of the role he had played in giving new emphasis to fiction merely posthumous encomiums. In 1859, attempting to appraise current trends in fiction, David Masson had been able to identify "a wholesome spirit of Realism" in the novels of the fifties, and he had claimed that this had resulted "to a great extent from the influence of Mr. Thackeray's example" (No. 403, p. 263).

Many of the retrospective appraisals were reiterative of elements that had been isolated for praise during Thackeray's lifetime—his realism, his role as moralist, the easy charm of his style. Some few of the articles, however, probed new veins. One of the best of these was a piece in the *Home and Foreign Review* by Richard Simpson that analyzed his work in terms of spiritual biography. Simpson's elaboration of what he called Thackeray's "theory of mitigated affections" came very close to isolating the basic response to life that did (and continues to) make Thackerayans of some readers and not of others (No. 485).

The most complete American attempt in 1864 to discuss Thackeray's work was the piece by Edwin Whipple, a critic who had strongly praised *Vanity Fair* when it had first appeared. Though Whipple still had praise for much of Thackeray's work, he found the qualities of the true "philosopher or poet" missing. As if to confirm this view, he used Thackeray's sympathy with the South in the Civil War to illustrate his indifference to truly great iniquities and his inability to see meaning and purpose beneath the surface of things (No. 482). Whipple's approach was but another instance of the extra-literary critical standards that were so often called into play, and it serves to recall that in America, particularly, national sentiment had served both to strengthen and at other times to weaken Thackeray's claim on the public.

During the two decades following his death the attempt was made to assign to Thackeray a permanent place in literature. Although the response to his work during these years seems subdued in comparison to the peak interest which he had created in the mid-fifties, many indices show an increase in popularity and critical estimation over that which he had enjoyed during the last few years of his life. His books were reprinted frequently, not only as separate volumes but in collected editions, the first of which appeared in England and America between 1867 and 1869. Through these decades a strong interest was also continually shown in any biographical information about him, and numerous personal memoirs and reminiscences were written, along with attempts at a full biography in spite of Thackeray's own injunction against one and his family's consequent refusal to authorize any.[19] Yet another example of the interest was the broadened range of articles about his work. Following James Hannay's "Studies on Thackeray," wherein he examined the writer as critic, essayist, poet, and satirist, as well as novelist (No. 507), many pieces were written which tried to explore special aspects of his work (e.g., the "Titmarsh" articles as art criticism, No. 570; the historical prototype for Barry Lyndon, No. 558). Not the least of Thackeray's assets was the ability of his work to attract a new generation of readers as well as maintaining the old; the essays that appeared in the undergraduate *Yale Literary Magazine*, for example, show the constant rediscovery of his work by young minds (Nos. 488, 524, 528, 534).

Thackeray's English publisher, Smith, Elder, brought out the DeLuxe Edition of his work in 1878-1879. Appended to the final volume was a long critical essay by Leslie Stephen that attempted to view Thackeray's work within the framework of literary history as well as examining individual works in some

19. See Ray, Introduction, I, pp. 1-9, for a full account of the history of Thackeray's biographies, including his reasons for not desiring one.

detail. A tone of reserve and impartial judgment informed the entire piece, especially the discussion of his insistent irony (No. 549), and the sense that the essay implicitly imparted was that Thackeray was on his way to becoming a classic, though certainly one with a current vitality. The *Times*, in a notice that reviewed this edition along with the works of Dickens, despite a preference for Dickens, was able to affirm that Thackeray's high place in the literature of the century "is acknowledged by the age we live in."[20] According to the *Athenaeum*, the "mirror of Victorian culture," Thackeray's "mixture of half-hearted pessimism and real optimism" was still in vogue. He was thought to be "the only novelist of his time . . . whose popularity is increasing. While his rivals are suffering from the reaction that always follows success, he has been steadily gaining ground. His mood is critical enough to suit the taste of the time, and not critical enough to injure his novels as works of art" (No. 550). That this may be doubtful praise is not in question. But it does tend to confirm once again the very close spiritual relation of Thackeray and the Victorian age.

From the early 1880's through the end of the century the base of Thackeray's popularity became still broader, though some dissident voices were raised, refurbishing old complaints as well as introducing new elements of critical dissatisfaction. The long-standing suspicion of Thackeray's personal snobbery, unallayed because of the lack of any complete biography, was permitted to take on new life after two renewed personal attacks on him. In 1880, Disraeli (long irritated by Thackeray's 1847 burlesque of *Coningsby*) published *Endymion*, in which the vain and idle novelist, St. Barbe, was taken immediately as a caricature of Thackeray. Capitalizing on the presentation of this adverse image, Edmund Yates, who bore his grudge against Thackeray from 1858, brought out a new article to prove that it was the novelist's snobbishness that had been responsible for the Gar-

20. *Times*, Sept. 16, 1879, p. 9.

rick Club Affair.[21] These personal rebukes in part inspired the
renewed critical objections that Thackeray's work tended to serve
the "gentlemanly interest," and, furthermore, that it suffered because his mind was "turbid and confused," unable to avert itself
from "social ambition and pride of position" (No. 554). To be
sure, such complaints were answered immediately (No. 555) as
well as in years to come, when, for example, Robert Louis Stevenson found Thackeray's connections with society the mainspring of his ability to portray truthfully—with petty faults and
even vulgarity at times—"gentlemen" in fiction (No. 592). To
some extent these concerns were repetitive of the older issue,
raised within his lifetime, regarding Thackeray's depiction of
only a limited aspect of life. But they also reflected signs of dis-
affection with certain Victorian values by younger men first coming into their own in the eighties. A more striking example of
such a conflict of outlooks was afforded by an American article
at the very end of the century. Henry Sedgwick's diatribe against
Thackeray as "the poet of respectability" rested on the fact that
he had not responded to the industrial revolution and taken a
positive position in attempting to rectify its evils. A fervent, if
not overzealous, egalitarianism ran through the article, and at
one point it is difficult to tell whether it was mere observation or
proletarian derisiveness which prompted him to say: "The *bour-
geoisie* have their epic in *Vanity Fair*" (No. 661).

Whereas Sedgwick's line of attack was illustrative of the nar-
rowly moralistic critic somehow modified by the changing times,
William Dean Howells' change of attitude, from unstinted praise
of Thackeray at mid-century to dissatisfaction thirty years later,
was more representative of the writers who were beginning to
discover how much of life literature had generally overlooked.
"The greatest talent," wrote Howells, "is not that which breathes
of the library, but that which breathes of the street, the field, the
open sky, the simple earth" (No. 626, p. 137). In effect, he felt

21. "An Old Club Scandal," *Time*, II (Jan. 1880), 385-392. For a com-
plete discussion of the events which forced Yates's expulsion from the Garrick
Club, see Ray, II, 278-290; and also Edgar Johnson, *Charles Dickens: His
Tragedy and Triumph* (New York, 1952), II, 930-936.

it necessary to disclaim kinship with the literary tone in Thackeray's work in order to identify himself with the new subject matter of realistic American fiction.

Indeed, it was Howells' need to promote whatever new literary fancy took hold of him that led him into his first public expression of adverse criticism of Thackeray. In 1882, in an article whose purpose was to praise and introduce Henry James, Howells included the following remarks: "The art of fiction has, in fact, become a finer art in our day than it was with Dickens and Thackeray. We could not suffer the confidential attitude of the latter now, nor the mannerism of the former, any more than we could endure the prolixity of Richardson or the coarseness of Fielding. These great men are of the past—they and their methods and interests."[22] It is clear from the full article that this single allusion to Thackeray and the older English writers was the result of Howells' strong efforts to promote a new aesthetic in fiction—one influenced by the French Realists and being practiced by James—and it was not meant to be taken as a carefully developed critique either of Thackeray or the other writers mentioned.

The public's angry response to the remarks about Dickens and Thackeray nevertheless was indicative of the regard they still held for these men, and Howells felt compelled to offer an apology, explaining that he was sure he had been misunderstood. "I always thought myself quite unapproachable in my appreciation of the great qualities of Dickens and Thackeray . . . . I suspect that no Englishman could rate them higher than I do."[23] But in spite of his attempt to gloss over the comments, there was deep resentment that any contemporary critic or novelist dared to imply that a writer of Thackeray's stature was, in effect, obsolete. *Life*, for example, published a cartoon which showed a large statue of Thackeray, beside which Henry James stood on Howells' shoulders, and he in turn stood on two volumes of the *Century*. Remarked Howells: "Are you the tallest now, Mr.

22. "Henry James, Jr.," *Century*, XXV (Nov., 1882), 28.
23. "Literary Gossip," *Athenaeum* (Nov. 25, 1882), p. 700.

J-mes?" To which James replied: "Be so uncommonly kind, H-w-lls, as to let me down easy: It may be we have both got to grow."[24]

The evidence thus seems to show that although new attitudes towards fictional technique and substance were appearing, they in no way toppled Thackeray from the pedestal he occupied. On the contrary, many new editions of his work in the late eighties and nineties indicate an expanding circle of readers. In 1887 Frederick Dolman was able to report that "Thackeray is now finding entrance to the humblest homes" (No. 575). And a book-news periodical noted in the following year that his work was more popular than when he died.[25] Numerous articles concerned with bibliographic problems and bibliographies of his earliest and uncollected writings reflected the growing interest, as did the several new attempts at a biography that were undertaken (Nos. 603, 648). When the *Academy* assessed his reputation at the turn of the century, it was found higher than that of most of his compeers. Not only had Thackeray survived but he had become a classic. The explanation that the article offered was that Thackeray's realism, though it had once needed to justify itself against other literary modes, had become the accepted standard—"Owing to Thackeray himself, literary ideals have changed" (No. 650). A similar estimate of his popularity was made in America in an article by Hamilton Mabie, "The Most Popular Novels in America," which was based on a survey of the books most called for in American libraries. Although Dickens' *David Copperfield* held top honors, *Vanity Fair* proved to be sixth in popularity, appearing on eighty per cent of the library lists. *The Newcomes, Esmond,* and *Pendennis* were less favored, though all three held respectable positions as the fortieth, forty-third, and sixty-eighth books on a list of 175. Mabie rightly pointed out, however, that the survey in no way took into account the fact that many books of great popularity were owned by readers, thus making library use of them unnecessary. He be-

24. *Life*, I (Feb. 22, 1883), 91.
25. J. Ashby-Sterry, "English Notes," *Book Buyer*, V (Feb., 1888), 11.

lieved that this was especially true of "classic fiction" such as that of Thackeray. In regard to *Vanity Fair*, Mabie was able to say that it was "probably the greatest story in our language .... It is, indeed, one of the authentic documents of human history."[26]

The criticism of the nineties lends credence to the general vogue that Thackeray enjoyed. This is not to say that there were no negative comments. There still existed people both in England (Nos. 619, 659) and America (Nos. 669, 689, 695) who found it impossible to accept Thackeray fully because of his moral or philosophic view of life. They found his world too sad, too evil, or too hopeless. Some were compelled to deny the essential truthfulness of his depictions altogether, while others granted the realism of his world but nevertheless found it unhappy and depressing. Another negative strain resulted from the line of criticism that Howells had merely suggested in 1882: that there was something inartistic in Thackeray's fictional technique, his digressive and analytical way of presenting the characters and the story. In the nineties other writers besides Howells reflected this concern with the aesthetics of fiction. Often, though aesthetics was not the principal subject of the criticism, it clearly underlay the judgments being made: for example, praise for *Barry Lyndon* because it avoided Thackeray's "native bias towards the didactic" (No. 643); or an analysis of Becky Sharp that pointed to a failure in Thackeray's integrity as an artist and as a realist, in that by trying to graft a moral on the story he made her odious when he knew in fact that she was not (No. 685). Howells himself also amplified his criticism of Thackeray's method, remarking that he "avoided a direct rendering of life," "talked of fiction as a fableland," and "formed the vicious habit of spoiling the illusion." But even while these very comments were being made, Howells could also note that Thackeray had in fact created women who embodied the "Ever-Womanly," and that "his art is quite unerring in result though it is mostly bad in process" (No. 697). This combination of high praise

26. *Forum*, XVI (Dec., 1893), 508-510, 513.

along with censure is revealing, not only in the case of Howells but also for the other critics who found grounds for complaint. Invariably they also found much to commend though they were unable often to explain how or why it was good.

The critic who best performed the task of explaining Thackeray's work as a novelist, William Brownell, based his argument on the fact that it was the "sense of life" that finally emerged from a work of fiction that counted most. Different techniques were not in themselves good or bad, but merely relative to the end result. He argued that though James's technique of "filling life around character" was good, Thackeray's analytical technique was equally reliable. In fact, it proved to be a "short cut to verisimilitude . . . by attuning the reader to the rhythm of the subject and establishing between them a mutuality of relationship," and this indeed was an important advantage for "the novel on a large scale" as Thackeray had understood and produced it (No. 674). Elsewhere Brownell analyzed Thackeray's work in terms that substantiated many of the comments in less complete critiques. He identified the writer's theme as the complexity of the moral element in character, and showed how, by drawing "character not merely in its elemental traits, but in its morally significant ones as well," Thackeray had created and criticized a whole society (No. 647).

As the century closed, it was evident that critics and bookmen shared with the great public an essential endorsement of Thackeray, and in retrospect his prestige appears to have been continuous. He had not merely ridden the crest of current fashion (as had other novelists of his day) but had been in touch with something more like the true spirit of an age. Perhaps, too, it would be well to consider that Thackeray represented a voice, a personality, a total response to life, which found disfavor with many but likewise for many others spoke a not uncommon refrain. In the days before the first success of *Vanity Fair*, a review in England had remarked of him: "He lets the reader into the secret of his own character" (No. 41). Another had noted: "He makes his book speak like a man" (No. 63). Fifty years later the same sentiments were possible. "When we think of him," wrote Wilbur Cross, "his asides and comments are what return oftenest upon the memory" (No. 677). And to Brownell, the total expression of Thackeray's work was the "outgrowth of the most interesting personality . . . that has expressed itself in prose" (No. 674).

It remained for the early years of the twentieth century, and the disdain of all things Victorian, to deflate Thackeray's reputation, first by attack and then by disregard. Though a revival of interest began in the 1940's and has continued up to the present, it has by no means restored to him the prestige he held at the end of the nineteenth century. Then, *Vanity Fair, Pendennis, Esmond,* and *The Newcomes* were the bastions of a reputation that embraced classic greatness and popularity.

2. *Critical Problems of Realism*

Certain generally held attitudes were the bases for much of the criticism of Thackeray's work. Whereas certain concepts, such as that of "plot" in fiction, were specifically literary in scope, others, like "realism," cast a wide net that brought in many social and moral viewpoints. The present discussion merely attempts to scratch the surface of an analysis of some of the attitudes relating to realism: firstly, with the hope of clarifying the ideas and terminology in the items in the bibliography; and, secondly, as a suggestion for the thematic organization of some of this material.

Some form or other of the idea of realism was a feature of almost all the criticism about Thackeray. The word "realism" itself, however, seems not to have been used before the fifties to indicate strictly a literary mode or movement. In 1851 Thackeray was called the "chief of the Realist School" (No. 139). No further elaboration was provided for this description, nor did the article discuss realism as a mode. Prior to this piece as well as after it, critics were more accustomed to describe the quality they had in mind each according to his own bent. "Fidelity to nature" and "representation of actual life" are two examples of such descriptions. Implicit in these formulations was the notion that the literary work reproduced reality almost to the point of doing away with the author's capacity for selection. Nor was any distinction made between realism of presentation and realism of assessment—between the way in which a story was told and the overall evaluative judgment concerning the subject matter of the story. Thus confusion was easily created in regard to romances, fables, and fantasies that were nevertheless couched in the most everyday language and works that conveyed a sense of reality though their techniques involved stylization, digression, imagery, and allusion uncommon to everyday language. Thackeray himself was highly critical of what he called "romances"—the works of Ainsworth, Bulwer, and G.P.R. James—and yet one of his most charming pieces. *The Rose and the Ring*, is, broadly speaking, romance. Though he could give no clear expression to his views in terms of the critical jargon of the day, what he really was objecting to were bad novels (as Henry James was to call these "romances" years later). Because of their verisimilitude they suggested the real world in the same way as did a novel, but the successes and failures of their characters were more in tune with wish-fulfilling fantasies. In this sense Thackeray along with many others thought of them as morally pernicious. It was their assessment of reality that fundamentally seemed to draw the censure. However, because of the failure to distinguish between presentation and assessment, Thackeray did not scruple at parodying the extremities of style of these "romances" in *Novels by Eminent Hands*. He did not trouble himself to consider whether, for example, Disraeli's mannerisms of language and stylized characters did not in the long run create an imitation (in the Aristotelian sense) of reality. Thackeray's own critical limitation in this respect was shared by other novelists of his time as well as by the practicing critics. Much of the criticism of his work must be understood in the light of this assumption.

In the attempt to come to grips with the term "realism" and with Thackeray's brand of it particularly, some critics found their footing by means of an analogy with the newly developed craft ("art") of photography, the great novelty of which was "its amazing literal reproduction." The comparison was anything but fortunate for literary realism. Thackeray's "habit of viewing life and reproducing it with an *impassive* and *mirror-like* [italics mine] fidelity" was identified as cynicism because of the "impersonal and unsympathetic point of view whence he regards his characters." Furthermore, it implied a failure in art because it reproduced detail without distinction (No. 421). This critique in 1860 seems to have been the implicit basis for certain reservations expressed about *Vanity Fair* twelve years earlier. The "life-like and natural" quality of that novel was nevertheless objectionable to some degree because it suggested "sketches of life" or "sketches of character," which did not seem in keeping with novels as they were known (No. 72). It was a "novel without a plan" that moved along just as "the progress of one's own life" (No. 75). Even a mid-century critic of some competence like William Roscoe was encumbered by this concept. He appraised Thackeray as a great "painter of manners," but this acclaim held the seeds of dispraise. The argument ran as follows: Although Thackeray might well be the greatest realist, he would only be the greatest novelist "if the power of producing the impression of reality were the test of the highest creative powers." Clearly, according to Roscoe, it was not. The realist only desired "to be a mirror" and as such could not produce true art (No. 359). Explicit in this critique is the notion of the realist's lack of creative imagination, and implicit is the ultimate emphasis on the subject matter of the literary work.

This emphasis on the details of the life represented without concern for the method of presentation can be seen even more clearly by glancing momentarily at certain remarks of William Dean Howells towards the end of the century. The main force of his complaint then was that Thackeray "formed the vicious habit of spoiling the illusion" of his work by rendering life circuitously, by employing a method of presentation that destroyed the sense of reality in his fiction (Nos. 626, 697). For Howells and for Henry James the difference between Thackeray and Flaubert was indeed great—the one intrusively identifying himself as creator, the puppeteer with his puppets, and the other submerged in the work itself, refraining from all direct comment. But this nice distinction between Thackeray's realism and *le Réalism* was not apparent in 1857 when Fitzjames Stephen reviewed *Madame Bovary* and was able to say that Flaubert's "style conveys to us the impression that it has been formed upon that of Mr. Thackeray of whose influence it shows the strongest traces."[27]

Another attempt at clarifying literary realism in the fifties was made by calling into play the old distinction of "real" and "ideal," specifically relating it to the art of painting. On the occasion of comparing Dickens with Thackeray, David Masson employed this dichotomy, pointing out that the "idealist" added elements that were not in the original living subject as well as giving special emphasis to others for the purpose of a desired imaginative effect (No. 148). This view, though admitting both the "real" and "ideal" as approaches to the creation of art, nevertheless again suggested a lack of creativity or imagination on the part of the realist. It also failed to suggest that the realistic work could just as easily be symbolic in the broadest sense. Indeed, the ability of moralistic critics as late as 1900 to find Becky Sharp a "Jezebel" figure and *Vanity Fair* a sort of moral fable (e.g., Nos. 689, 695) indicates that realistic detail in the novel did function as something more than reportage.

Critics were not alone in this confusion of methods with the final expression a work achieved. Thackeray's own artistic creed seemingly took cognizance of the "real-ideal" division, and like the critics he theoretically denied the symbolic function of objects, characters, and events. In a letter to Masson, he indicated his dislike of fiction that did not represent "Nature duly." "In a drawing room drama a coat is a coat and a poker a poker; and must be nothing else according to my ethics."[28] It was very im-

---

27. *Saturday Review*, IV (July 11, 1857), 40-41.
28. *Letters*, II, 772-773.

portant for Thackeray to make his approach understood, because he was trying to use the argument of truthfulness in order to defend the selfishness or meanness of his characters, and to this end he asked Whitwell Elwin to make these intentions clear. Elwin's article indeed attempted to do so. After first pointing out that most other novelists "describe characters under exceptional circumstances, . . . influenced by passions which seldom operate in their excess with each individual, and . . . actors in adventures which . . . happen to few or none," Elwin went on to assert that "Thackeray looks at life under its ordinary aspects, and copies it with a fidelity and artistic skill which are surprising. Men, women, and children talk, act, and think in his pages exactly as they are talking, acting, and thinking at every hour of every day" (No. 321). Basically this was a defense of literature on the grounds that a story and its details were true. And though this may seem an inadequate defense, it was one also made by Dickens when charged with being something other than a realist in the sense just discussed. George Ford, commenting on Dickens' declaration that certain things in his work were "true," has pointed to the lameness of this defense by recalling that in the eighteenth century Fielding had been able to quote Aristotle as saying that it is no excuse that the incredible is declared to have actually happened.[29] The idea, understood since classical literature, that art always entails conventions seemed to have been lost sight of in regard to fiction. Some concept of poetic or artistic truth was the thing most needed to temper the debate about realism.

In the hope of at least offsetting the misconception about the lack of imagination on the part of the realist, Elwin attempted an answer: "A notion prevails that to keep thus closely to reality precludes imagination, as if it was possible to furnish an entire novel—plot, person, and conversations—exclusively or mainly from memory. The difference between him who wanders in fancy's maze, and him who stoops to truth, is not that the one creates and the other copies, but that the first goes further than

29. *Dickens and His Readers* (Princeton, N. J., 1955), p. 132.

nature and the second invents in obedience to its laws (No. 321)."

The inadequacies of this explanation are only too evident. Though recognizing the creative function of both kinds of writers, Elwin's distinction could only serve to separate almost all professed novelists from a handful who would readily agree that they had gone "further than nature," because they had meant their work to be fantasy or fable. The distinction hardly could prove useful for analyzing the difference between Thackeray and Dickens, and these writers invariably became the focus of discussions of realism. The confusion seemed to turn, time and again, on the unacknowledged difference between the subject matter of the work and what was wrought from this material; and criticism continued, year after year, to deny symbolic function to the realistic mode.

An example of this tendency was the analogy that was drawn between Thackeray's fiction and the Pre-Raphaelite group of artists. His work was seen as "a pre-Raphaelite school of novel writing," merely a reaction to false idealism, a deflating force, that could not be valued as art in itself (No. 387). Other critiques that identified the relation of Thackeray and the young painters and poets were less quick to censure and often merely avoided any evaluation of the approach as a form of art (e.g., No. 403, p. 267). It was enough for these critics to point to the "scrupulous fidelity to nature, or extreme accuracy in minute detail," that connected the fiction with the paintings (No. 494). But, once this supposed relationship was established, the inference could be made that a fiction of realism suffered the same faults as the work of the Pre-Raphaelites—it aspired no higher than to be an unqualified duplication of reality. And though Thackeray may not have been willing or able to defend his work on grounds other than its "fidelity to nature," the Pre-Raphaelite "reverence for accurate reproduction was from the first qualified by a desire that each detail fully realized might stand as a symbol of some spiritual force above sense perception."[30] Thus, the mis-

30. Jerome H. Buckley, *The Victorian Temper* (New York, 1964), p. 164.

understanding of Pre-Raphaelite art can be seen as paralleling the limiting idea of realism that was applied to fiction.

The emphasis that was placed on factual truth (rather than on artistic truth) suggests that the final standards of criticism tended to be ones external to the fictional work. The task of appraisal became one of evaluation in terms of social or moral dicta. If the realistic mode was thought to contain little or no art how could its accomplishment be judged except in terms of how faithful it had been to reality? And to judge this quality a critic needed to have a particular idea of reality in mind. Much of the praise as well as the dispraise of Thackeray as a moralist rested on the individual critic's sense of reality. To be sure, there were some who glimpsed something of the autonomy of a work of art, but this thought was a threatening one and quickly led them to the conclusion that if artistic truth alone was the end of art, then novels were really "unfit for the purpose of discussing serious subjects."[31] This view, however, was a minority one. Much more common was the emphasis on the didactic role that fiction could fulfill—the theory of the sugar-coated pill. Realistic fiction particularly was serviceable to this end since one could ultimately defend its conclusions on the grounds of the actual truth of its details. Much of the praise of *Vanity Fair* was founded upon just such judgments (e.g., Nos. 69, 82). At best, however, this kind of criticism left itself open to the challenge that the critic had a mistaken view of reality.

It was this difference in world-views that categorized the three principal strains of Thackeray critics within his lifetime. There were those who accepted him as a realist whose satire was aimed at moral correction, others who granted his realism but objected to the cynicism it entailed, and, finally, those who denied the truth of his depiction on the grounds that his world was too evil to be representative of the real world. These categories indeed represent a simplification, since there were many shades of difference even among those who agreed with each other.

31. [James Fitzjames Stephen], "Novels and Novelists," *Saturday Review*, VI (Sept. 18, 1858), 285-286.

Fundamentally, however, the division is a sound one. But what seems more important to observe is the persistence of these categories throughout the century—the persistence of the concept that realism involved an all-inclusive photograph of the world, especially the world known to the individual critic. Even among those men seemingly concerned with the aesthetics of fiction, final recourse was sought by calling upon an essentially personal view of reality. Adolphus Jack argued that *Vanity Fair* was immoral because it was inartistic and inartistic because life could not be as Thackeray had depicted it (No. 624). Similarly, it was the attitude towards life inherent in Thackeray's work that barred Howells from a full appreciation of the fiction at the close of the century. It was the "unhandsome dénouement" of *Esmond* which troubled him, for example, Rachel's unlovely marriage which did "not seem either nice or true" (No. 698). In effect, Howells was saying that Thackeray's work did not illustrate "the smiling aspects of life" which he had come to believe were the more fit subjects for novelists.

The bias that prevented an individual from recognizing the realistic mode for what it was, as something distinct from any approval of the aspect of reality dealt with, was not restricted to personal attitudes alone. Nationalist sentiment often could and did intrude, sometimes with the effect of admitting the realism of a foreign work, and sometimes rejecting it, but most frequently for the purpose of proving something about the other country rather than something about the literary work. The realism of Balzac, Sand, Flaubert, and Zola throughout the Victorian age confirmed the English in their notions of French depravity, primarily because of the relatively frank portrayals of sex relationships. When works of these authors were admitted to be works of realism, it became necessary to draw conclusions about the moral state of French society. Thackeray himself, as his earliest magazine pieces show, was guilty of publicizing this British prejudice against French literature (See No. 566), though indeed much of his own early fiction created a world of just such petty self-servers as he found in Balzac's work.

In much the same way that the English were only able to recognize the realism of French authors by ascribing certain conditions to French life, American critics from time to time appraised British fiction by the same method. For some, Thackeray's world could more easily be accepted as realistic because its immorality was English and not American; it in no way affronted the American self-image. Charles Bristed thought it "most hateful" that a woman could neglect her child as Becky Sharp did, but he was quick to add that "in this country, we are proud to say, it *is* an impossibility" (No. 78). The sense of moral superiority was even stronger in an article of 1852: "The author's satire on titled insipidity and servility in the lower classes is positively savage; and from this, as from all Thackeray's work, one takes up the impression that English society is rotten to the core" (No. 195).

Whether it was nationalism, religion, or a private moral outlook that governed the appraisal of the representation of reality, the effect remained the same. The realism of the work was gauged by how closely it approximated a reality compatible to that of the critic; and no English critical formulations of realism in the nineteenth century, a period when modern realism truly came of age, treated it as a literary method viable in its own terms, with distinct boundaries between it and other modes. In mitigation of the problematic effects of thinking of realism merely as "scrupulous fidelity to nature," some were able to sense even in the fifties that it was a "spirit" in literature as well as a result (No. 403). In the nineties this same view was given voice when realism was identified as an "expression of a mood" (No. 677). But no American or English critic of Thackeray's work developed this notion to the point of being able to answer the frequent charges that he only depicted a small part of reality, and the less pretty part at that. In the present century, Carl Van Doren was to say, "Realism . . . is a matter of the realist's intention rather than of his success or failure. He cannot be a clear window through which all reality may be seen, for the reason that reality is too vast."[32] As simple as this may sound today, no equivalent defense was made for Thackeray by his contemporaries.

Thackeray, then, as a point of focus provides the means by which we can examine the thinking of an era in terms of its social and ethical tenets, as well as in regard to its theories of literature. For the student of Thackeray's fiction there yet remains the task of exploring his methods *qua* novelist, and many leads into this study are provided through an understanding of how Thackeray was read by his contemporaries. The bibliography that follows, presenting the full range of British and American criticism of Thackeray's work in the nineteenth century, was prepared in order to provide a springboard for such research. The method of annotation attempts to present the tone and substance of the items without prejudicial alteration, thus permitting the critics to speak for themselves. These articles and books that were written—whether thoughtful or hastily contrived, because of what they said or even what they failed to say—provide a rich source for further analysis.

32. "American Realism," *New Republic*, XXXIV (March 21, 1923), 107.

THE BIBLIOGRAPHY

Scope and Organization

This bibliography lists and annotates (subject to the limitations and methods noted below) the critical and biographical books and articles on Thackeray in England and the United States from 1836 to 1901.

Completeness and accuracy were the goal of this work. Entries are the result of a search that attempted to investigate all leads at each step of the way. From time to time citations of pertinent items were found in works not about Thackeray but dealing, for example, with the history of a magazine or with the career of one of his contemporaries. However, the main direction of the search proceeded along the following lines:

> The *CBEL* and the 1957 Supplement were examined and all bibliographical, biographical, and critical entries for Thackeray listed therein were searched in turn. To these works may be added *The Library of William D. Lambert*: Part III— Thackerayana (New York, 1914); Gordon N. Ray, *Thackeray*, 2 vols. (New York, 1955-1958); Sara Carruth, "Thackeray's Critical Reputation in England, 1840-1903," Unpublished Ph.D. dissertation, Univ. of Chicago, 1958; Helen McCarthy, "Thackeray and Serialization," Unpublished Ph.D. dissertation, Columbia University, 1961.

These sources were principally supplemented by:

> Catalogs of the New York Public Library, the Columbia University Library, the Library of Congress, and the Library of the British Museum;
> National bibliographies such as the *English Catalogue* and the various American catalogs—Kelly, Roorbach, Bowker's

American Catalogue, and the *United States Catalog*: Books in Print;
Allibone's Critical Dictionary of English Literature; *Dictionary of National Biography*;
Periodical indexes such as *Poole's* and *Readers' Guide*; and the New York University (card) Index to Early American Periodical Literature: 1728-1870;
Cumulative indexes of individual periodicals and newspapers. When indexes were not available and a paucity of criticism seemed to betray oversight, the better-known publications were searched issue by issue.

Of some 1500 items referring to Thackeray which were examined, approximately 675 were omitted on the basis of the exclusions below, primarily numbers 3, 4, 5, and 9. Among the 875 items selected for inclusion, about 175 proved to be reprints.

Exclusions from the bibliography:

1. Editions and reprints of Thackeray's work, including editors' prefaces and introductions, except when such editorial material is of critical significance. (See Note A below.)
2. Dramatizations and summaries of the novels.
3. Books and articles exclusively concerning bibliographical problems.
4. Accounts in literary histories which do not devote a separate chapter to Thackeray and/or his work, except where the literary history in question is a major reference work or has historical importance.
5. Brief and anonymous material from publishers' lists and trade journals, and announcements of publication in other periodicals and newspapers.
6. Reviews and notices of 2, 3, 4, and 5 above.
7. Most encyclopedia accounts.
8. Newspaper articles and reviews other than those contemporary with Thackeray's life.
9. Allusions and ana. (See Note B below.)

Notes concerning the exclusions:

A. For a detailed bibliography of Thackeray's own work, see Vol. II, 143-376, of Lewis Melville's *Life of William*

Makepeace Thackeray (London, 1910); and for American editions exclusively, Frederick S. Dickson's bibliography in Vol. II, 229-294, of James G. Wilson's *Thackeray in the United States* (London, 1904).

B. Principal biographical studies are listed in the bibliography; however, personal memoirs, anecdotal accounts, and biographical sketches which treat of Thackeray but briefly are not listed unless these items in some way include critical comment. The full range of this material is well accounted for in a biographical sense by Gordon N. Ray's *Thackeray*, 2 vols. (New York, 1955-1958).

Organization of the bibliography:

The order of entries is chronological. However, the following modifications of this method should be noted:

1) The notices of Thackeray's lectures in the years 1851, 1852, 1853, 1855, 1856, and 1857 are grouped together in each of these years. Similarly, the notices of the Brookfield letters are grouped together in the years 1887 and 1888.

2) A series of articles that are in effect one, though published in different issues of a periodical, are treated as one entry. This holds true even in the case where the later installments were published in a different year.

3) Allowance must be made for a periodical or book whose date of publication can only be fixed in terms of a specific month. In such a case the publication date is presumed to be the first of the month unless internal evidence indicates that the item appeared earlier or later, in which case it is so placed.

4) When two or more entries have the same date of publication and internal evidence does not indicate sequential order, a book precedes a periodical and periodicals are ordered alphabetically by name.

5) In a few cases the month of publication of a book was not determined. These items are identified by a dagger (†) before their entry numbers.

Items are entered according to the date of original publication, and all subsequent reprintings, either in periodicals or books, are listed under the one entry.

Names of periodicals and newspapers are given as they were at the time the item was published in spite of later changes.

A name common to different concurrent publications is clarified by its place of publication. When *place* is not indicated in such ambiguous cases, London is to be presumed.

Periodicals are distinguished from newspapers by the use of parentheses around the date of the issue, as well as by the appearance of volume numbers in roman numerals preceding the date. However, in those cases where the magazine does not have volume numbers (e.g., *Examiner, Athenaeum*), the parentheses alone serves to make the identification.

Index:

A separate index, which follows the bibliography, locates items according to their authors, the individual works of Thackeray discussed, and also according to certain categories of critical interest.

Attributions:

The principal authorities for the attribution of unsigned articles are as follows: Thackeray's *Letters and Private Papers*, edited by Gordon N. Ray, 4 vols. (Cambridge, Mass., 1945-1946); Gordon N. Ray, *Thackeray*, 2 vols. (New York, 1955-1958); Leslie Marchand, *The Athenaeum: A Mirror of Victorian Culture* (Chapel Hill, N. C., 1941); James G. Wilson, *Thackeray in the United States*, 2 vols. (London, 1904), including Frederick S. Dickson's bibliography in Volume II; Samuel A. Allibone, *Critical Dictionary of English Literature*, 3 vols. (Philadelphia, 1871); Frank L. Mott, *A History of American Magazines*, 4 vols. (Cambridge, Mass., 1938); *Poole's Index to Periodical Literature*; *Readers' Guide*; *CBEL*; The Wellesley Index; and the collections of essays and letters, where available, of the individual authors concerned.

Symbols:

* before entry number indicates an item of critical interest and/or importance.
† before entry number indicates a book for which the month of publication was not determined.
[ ] around entry number indicates that the item, as cited, was not examined.
[ ] around author's name indicates attributed authorship of unsigned articles.
A after entry number indicates a periodical, newspaper, or book published in the United States.

B after entry number indicates a periodical, newspaper, or book published in Great Britain.

Abbreviations:

The abbreviations below are used throughout the bibliography, including quotations, except where the names are part of the entry's title.

T	*William Makepeace Thackeray*
AP	*The Adventures of Philip*
BL	*The Memoirs of Barry Lyndon; The Luck of Barry Lyndon*
C	*Catherine*
CC	*Notes of a Journey from Cornhill to Grand Cairo*
DB	*Doctor Birch and His Young Friends*
DD	*Denis Duval*
E	*The History of Henry Esmond*
EH	*The English Humourists of the Eighteenth Century*
FB	*The Fitz-Boodle Papers; Confessions of Fitz-Boodle*
FG	*The Four Georges*
GHD	*The History of Samuel Titmarsh & the Great Hoggarty Diamond*
ISB	*The Irish Sketch Book*
JD	*Jeames's Diary; Diary of C. Jeames de la Pluche, Esq.*
K	*The Kickleburys on the Rhine*
L	*Lovel the Widower*
MG	*Some Passages in the Life of Major Gahagan; Major Gahagan's Reminiscences*
MPB	*Mrs. Perkins's Ball*
MW	*Men's Wives*
N	*The Newcomes*
NEH	*Novels by Eminent Hands; Punch's Prize Novelists*
OS	*Our Street*
P	*The History of Pendennis*
PSB	*The Paris Sketch Book*
RP	*Roundabout Papers*
RR	*The Rose and the Ring*
Reb	*Rebecca and Rowena*
S	*The Book of Snobs; The Snobs of England*
SFN	*The Second Funeral of Napoleon*
SGS	*A Shabby Genteel Story*
V	*The Virginians*
VF	*Vanity Fair*
YP	*The Yellowplush Correspondence; The Yellowplush Papers*

Bibliography

1836

1.B *Literary Gazette*, XX (April 30), 282-283.
Brief review of *Flore et Zephyr*. "One of the liveliest perceptions of the ridiculous . . . , and does infinite credit to the talents of the artist."

1838

2.A [Clark, Lewis G.]. "Editor's Table." *Knickerbocker*, XII (Sept.), 274-278; Rptd. *New Yorker*, VI (Sept. 29), 19-20.
Extracts from YP (Phila.), accompanying a complimentary summary of the book.

3.A *Evening Star* (New York), V, Sept. 20, Fol. 2; Rptd. *New Yorker*, VI (Sept. 22), 13.
The humor of YP (Phila.) is compared to that of *Humphrey Clinker*, and the domestic descriptions are likened to the work of "the immortal Boz."

4.A *Gentleman's Magazine* (Phila.), III (Oct.), 284.
Brief notice of YP (Phila.), praising the original, witty, and "quaint vileness of cacography."

1839

*5.A [Willis, Nathaniel P.]. "Jottings Down in London." *Corsair*, I (Aug. 24), 376.

Biographical sketch of T, introducing him as a new contributor. He "is one of the most accomplished draftsmen in England, as well as the cleverest and most brilliant of periodical writers."

1840

6.B "A Glance at the Periodicals." *Spectator*, XIII (Jan. 4), 17.
Brief notice of a new Yellowplush article (*Fraser's*, XXI, 71-80) re Bulwer, remarking the soundness of T's criticisms and "the playful, yet cutting ridicule."

7.B *Times*, July 17, p. 6.
PSB praised for its humor, and especially its restraint in caricature. Descriptions follow "closely to nature," indicating greater reliance on recollection than on "creative capacity."

8.B *Spectator*, XIII (July 18), 689.
Brief notice of PSB, praising its cleverness. But "the flippant ... style is not fit ... for continuous reading," and the satirical humor "is too severe and biting to be pleasant."

9.B [Forster, John]. *Examiner* (July 19), pp. 451-452.
Review of PSB. "Beatrice Merger" is "remarkable for its pathos and simplicity," just as "Meditations at Versailles" is "for its thoughtful truth and fiery sarcasm."

10.B *Athenaeum* (July 25), pp. 589-590.
PSB praised for its sketches of ordinary people, though T is too "free and easy" with the world of "musk, amber, and Japan," and too flippant for the "world of philosophers."

11.B *Atlas*, July 25, pp. 488-489.
PSB commended as an informal guide to Paris. T "is a humorist of the first water" and "a professed hater of humbug."

12.B *Literary Gazette*, XXIV (July 25), 474-476.
PSB shows a "keen sense of the ridiculous and a hostility to humbug."

1841

13.B *Britannia*, II (Jan. 9), 26.
SFN is a "small, but very amusing, and very meritorious work," written for "all who have any relish for wit."

14.B *Athenaeum* (Jan. 16), pp. 52-53.
SFN's opening passages suggest an exposé or satire, "but it turns out to be a mere (though very imperfect) newspaper report of the proceedings." Its defect is that it is "neither jest nor earnest."

15.B *Literary Gazette*, XXV (Jan. 16), 33-35.
SFN praised as "a curious mixture of the serio-jocose." As either artist or writer, "few can compare with . . . Titmarsh."

16.B [Forster, John]. *Examiner* (Jan. 17), p. 37.
Brief notice of SFN, commending it as "sensible, instructive, amusing."

*17.B *Times*, Jan. 19, p. 3.
Review of SFN. The antithesis of the "grave historian" and the facetious observer is not resolved, giving "the book the appearance of not being all of a piece." When T shows up humbug, "it is rather as a pleasant bagatelle than as a great cause of indignation."

18.B *Literary Gazette*, XXV (April 24), 260-261.
Brief notice of *Comic Tales and Sketches*. This collection is welcomed, in spite of a general disapproval of republication of periodical material.

19.A "Memorials of Gormandizing." *New World*, III (July 3), 13.
Short note identifies T as author of "Memorials of Gormandizing" (rptd. from *Fraser's* on p. 3 of this issue of *New World*), YP, and PSB.

1842

20.A [Clark, Lewis G.]. "Editor's Table." *Knickerbocker*, XIX (May), 485-488.
Comic Tales and Sketches commended. MG has "forcible and truthful satire." M. A. Titmarsh identified as T.

1843

21.B [Blanchard, Laman]. *Ainsworth's Magazine*, III (May), 435-438.
Review of ISB, praising T's drawings as well as his writing. "A rare work, both sad and humourous . . .—the humour uppermost, and the tender thoughtful sadness underneath."

22.B [Morgan, Sydney, Lady]. *Athenaeum* (May 13), pp. 455-457.
Review of ISB. T is fundamentally unable to grasp a "perfect understanding of the 'case of Ireland.' " Though honest, he is far from unprejudiced. In spite of this, he has ability to faithfully observe manners and personalities.

23.B *Literary Gazette*, XXVII (May 13), 314-316; (May 20), 334-335; (May 27), 350-351.
Brief complimentary notices of ISB. T "is an original," and this makes a reader gladly accept "either the solid information" or "the freaks and outbreaks of whim and fancy." (314) He can be pathetic and poetical as well as humorous. (351)

24.B *Tablet*, IV (May 13), 291-292.
ISB "has a subjective but not an objective truth. [T] doesn't falsify his impressions, but his impressions are false, . . . [because he] is an English Liberal, a thorough Cockney, a Protestant, a hater of controversy . . . and Repeal." The reader is in doubt whether his opinions are set forth seriously.

25.B *Spectator*, XVI (May 20), 471-472.
ISB "presents the best idea of Ireland and the Irish that we have met with," though it refrains from serious inquiry into political, social, or religious problems. There is some forced smartness and even "passages . . . that partake of the claptrap sentimentality of the man about town." T's cleverness permits him to "draw pleasantry from anything."

26.B *Morning Chronicle*, May 23, p. 5.
Review of ISB. T is "without prejudices and can appreciate all . . . the true virtues of such a people. . . . He has caught the very characteristics of the clime." However, "there is a

vein of pleasantry . . . which may not be quite palatable to some."

*27.B [Lever, Charles]. *Dublin University Magazine*, XXI (June), 647-657.
Review of ISB which makes effort to praise in spite of misgivings. T was wise enough not to propose "any very lofty object," but to limit his observations to "a tourist's sphere of vision." He arrived without preconceptions; however, "a desire for even-handed justice . . . leads him into the common error of attacking both sides"—priest-parson, landlord-tenant, Whigs-Tories.

28.B [Leigh, Percival]. "Titmarsh's Travels in Ireland." *Fraser's Magazine*, XXVII (June), 678-686.
Review of ISB, recommending it for its acute and unprejudiced observation, as well as its awareness of Ireland's misfortunes. "Melancholy and humor [are] quaintly blended."

29.B *Illuminated Magazine*, I (June), 118-119.
ISB is "the best book yet written upon Ireland." The picture is neither glossed nor sweetened. "Sympathy for the suffering, and . . . indignation towards injustice" help make the book a "great advance upon anything" T has done before.

30.B *Tait's Edinburgh Magazine*, N.S. X (June), 391-405.
ISB succeeds as a book "that should amuse." A few thrusts are aimed at T's inability to enjoy an Irish beggar's wit, to see real social problems, and to "respond to the sublime" in nature.

31.B "Ireland & Her Grievances." *Dublin Review*, XV (Aug.), 148-168.
ISB, purportedly reviewed along with two other books, receives little attention. It is noted that ISB does not look closely into the political, social, and economic problems with which this article is concerned.

1846

32.B *Athenaeum* (Jan. 24), pp. 89-91; (Jan. 31), pp. 118-120; Rptd. *Living Age*, VIII (March 21), 556-562.
CC is as it should be—"light as air. . . . It is to be read run-

ning, as it was written." (89) Regarding T's debunking of the wonders of the East, the reviewer asks: "Though he may pride himself on being honest and 'impartial,' is he not a little 'stony hearted'?" (120).

33.B "Titmarsh's Notes." *Literary Gazette*, XXX (Jan. 24), 75-77.
Review of CC. T's style is unique in that "as we laugh we gather wisdom." The book will "please and entertain every class of reader."

34.B *Spectator*, XIX (Jan. 24), 88-89.
Review of CC. T does not "subdue his own impressions out of deference to the majority. . . . The reader gets, perhaps not always the whole and lofty truth, but the actuality."

35.B *Morning Chronicle*, Jan. 29, pp. 5-6.
CC exhibits T's "contagious geniality" as well as his "power of recording *genuine* impressions, as distinct from *conventional* ones." It "is the most vivid, genial, pleasant book of travelling impressions . . . since *Eothen*."

36.B *Examiner* (Jan. 31), pp. 68-69; Rptd. *Living Age*, VIII (March 21), 553-556.
CC "is the book of an artist, not an adventurer . . . , of sights and pictures and the thoughts that play around them." It is full of "wonder and enchantment."

37.B "The Book of the Month." *Almanack of the Month*, I (Feb.), 106-107.
CC is "the best record of Mediterranean and Eastern impressions that we have ever read." "Fidelity and force of description" make it such, as well as "tolerant appreciation of men and manners different from our own."

38.B "Michael Angelo Titmarsh in the East." *New Monthly Magazine*, LXXVI (Feb.), 240-243.
Review of CC. T is at his best when describing in detail a particular place or incident that is not associated with past history nor with great pomp. His sneering at those things "which time and associations have taught us to love" is probably merely a pose.

39.B *Tablet,* VII (Feb. 7), 88-89.
CC presents a spirit "occasionally of spleen, sometimes of prejudice and bigotry . . . , but at its best, it speaks in tones of genuine humour." Reviewer forbears over-criticizing the "tainted portions" where T sneers at holy things, because there is "much wholesome food."

40.B *Morning Post,* Feb. 9, p. 6.
CC presents a "delightful diversity of entertainment . . . [in which] flashes of warmheartedness, goodness, and generosity . . . gleam through all this badinage and ribaldry."

41.B *Daily News,* Feb. 14, p. 7.
CC, though light reading, "contains matter to make the reader *think.*" T, like Pepys, Carlyle, Thomas Browne, and Robert Burton, exhibits his humor *in propria persona;* "he lets the reader into the secret of his own character."

42.B *Guardian* (Feb. 18), pp. 76-79.
Review of CC. T's descriptive power is granted, but "his real want of seriousness, his shallow, callous, infidel trifling" betrays his basic irreverence.

43.B *Douglas Jerrold's Shilling Magazine,* III (March), 277-278.
CC has "not only vivid pictures of foreign places and people, but that quiet, agreeable, good-humored satire on men and follies."

44.B *Tait's Edinburgh Magazine,* N.S. XIII (March), 199.
CC imparts "freshness and grace to things in themselves . . . homely, hackneyed, coarse, or trivial." But "cleverly as the task is gone through . . . the travesty is almost overdone— the book wants seriousness and earnestness, were it but for relief."

45.B *Times,* April 8, p. 7.
CC "is perfectly delightful . . . , peeping here and there . . . with our gay and light-hearted friend." But "with all its apparent levity, a strong undercurrent of good sense and right feeling."

46.B *Athenaeum* (Dec. 19), pp. 1290-1291.
Review of MPB. T "spares nobody; not even himself." "No element of a middle-class rout has been overlooked."

47.B *Examiner* (Dec. 19), pp. 804-805.
MPB is the work of a "true humorist and nice observer of character," and is "excellently suited to the [Christmas] season."

48.B *Morning Chronicle*, Dec. 29, p. 5.
MPB is outstanding among Christmas books. It is "the very embodiment of keen, shrewd common sense; . . . a perfect reflex of London middle-class society." T's "peculiarly suggestive" writing is executed with "perfect simplicity of style and manner."

1847

49.B "Christmas Books." *Dublin University Magazine*, XXIX (Jan.), 134-140.
Review of MPB. Offense is taken at the portrayal of Mulligan. T is rhetorically asked why he "should blurt out his stupid Cockney venom" against the Irish. Consequently, the rest of the book "is filled with a stupid repetition of frivolous and unmeaning details."

50.B *New Monthly Magazine*, LXXIX (Jan.), 142.
Brief review of MPB, alluding to its portrayal of "people whom everybody knows"—figuratively.

51.B "*The Battle of Life* and *Mrs. Perkins's Ball*." *Tait's Edinburgh Magazine*, N.S. XIV (Jan.), 55-60.
MPB "is vastly superior . . . as a story for Christmas or for any other season." It is "replete with broad and genuine humour and pointed sarcasm."

52.B *Lloyd's Weekly*, Jan. 3, p. 8.
Brief review of MPB. Dry humor, quiet satire, and shrewd common sense are present, as in all T's work. "His object has been to satirize the follies . . . of London middle-class society—the tillocracy; and he has succeeded admirably."

53.B *People's Journal*, III (Jan. 16), 39-40.
MPB praised for its character-drawing power.

*54.B [Masson, David]. "Popular Serial Literature." *North British Review*, VII (May), 110-136.
Notice of first 3 nos. of VF. T, though probably incapable of "delineating deep feelings" as Dickens can, writes in a "far purer style both of thought and expression. . . ." The tone of the sketches is "singularly tame and un-romantic," the characters, "milk-and-water rascals." Jane Austen constructed stories and plots whereas T does "not weave *stories* out of common things, but leaves common things as he finds them, and for effect, sketches clever pictures of the oddities of life."

*55.B *Sun*, June 10, Fol. 2.
Notice of No. 6 of VF. "If Mr. T were by some unforseen accident to die to-morrow his name would be transmitted down to posterity . . . by his VF. . . . He is the Fielding of the nineteenth century."

56.B [Chorley, Henry F.]. *Athenaeum* (July 24), pp. 785-786; Rptd. *Daguerreotype*, I (Oct. 16), 285-287.
Notice of first 7 nos. of VF. T is called a good-humored preacher. The power of the tale lies in Becky, for whom "we feel a sort of pity . . . and thus . . . complain that such a central figure is so set round with sensuality, gluttony, hypocrisy, and pretence." If VF fails to take permanent hold of the public, it will be because of T's preference "for the unpleasing and not because he fails in force of portraiture and in probability of dialogue. . . ."

1848

57.B [Hayward, Abraham]. "Thackeray's Writings." *Edinburgh Review*, LXXXVII (Jan.), 46-67; Rptd. *Living Age*, XVI (Feb. 5), 271-280.
ISB, CC, S, and MPB are briefly commented on, along with biographical information about T. But the general estimate rests largely on VF (first 11 nos.) which is "immeasurably superior" to all previous work. In it, one finds "freedom from mannerism and affectation both in style and sentiment,"

and a balance of good and evil in the characters. Also, there are no political theories put forward. Thanks are given to T for providing a "plain old-fashioned love story." (*sic*)

58.B *People's Journal*, V, 51-53.
OS praised for its insights into character and the descriptions of persons and places.

59.B *Britannia*, IX (Jan. 1), 10-11.
OS is both amusing and instructive. "T [is] . . . one of our best comic writers." His work bears comparison to that of Molière. Its end is to satirize "the vulgar pretension which . . . commonly characterizes middle-life," and which deserves even harsher treatment than T's.

60.B *Douglas Jerrold's Weekly*, Jan. 1, pp. 13-14.
Review of OS. "T's descriptions are so exact, and his portraits so true, that we can only award him the merit of an historian. . . . He is a social commentator worthy of Machiavelli or Michelet."

61.B *Examiner* (Jan. 1), p. 4.
OS is an "audacious little book," in that it reveals everybody's "secrets and privacies," though it does so in a good-natured way.

62.B *Literary Gazette*, XXXII (Jan. 1), 12.
Brief notice of OS. "The sketches are slight, but full of life and reality."

63.B *Morning Chronicle*, Jan. 5, Fols. 3-4.
Review of OS. The charm of T's writing is that it is like talking—"pleasant, sunny, half-trifling, half-earnest chat—in fact, a sort of wise man's prattle. . . . He makes his book speak like a man."

64.B *Athenaeum* (Jan. 8), pp. 36-37.
OS is an improvement over MPB. "A touch of the Poet . . . [in T] raises him far above the mere maker of a 'fool born jest.' " His work, however, would not suffer if he were less sparing in sentiment.

65.B *Times*, Jan. 11, p. 8.
OS follows the plan laid out in MPB, "that of sketching a variety of characters, without . . . a story. . . ." But OS provides fuller descriptions, though T is still concise. He is a master of irony, and "his constant aim in OS and in MPB and S is to *show up* the difference between what people are and what they are striving . . . to appear to be." But "he plays with the humbug of society as though he regarded it as a weakness rather than a vice."

66.B *John Bull*, XXVIII (Jan. 15), 43.
OS better than MPB in all respects. T "possesses the power of delineating characters by a few striking points of resemblance, instead of minute description."

67.B *Tait's Edinburgh Magazine*, N.S. XV (Feb.), 140-141.
OS commended for both drawings and text.

68.B [Lewes, George H.]. *Morning Chronicle*, March 6, p. 3.
Review of S, though largely a general discussion of T's work with illustrations from VF. (The main points are recast more fully in No. 73 below.) In S the satire is impartial. T does not flatter the reader, but includes him in the satire.

69.B *Tablet*, IX (July 1), 426.
Review of Nos. 1-18 of VF. Previous work did not show T's genius. The "spirit of utter worldliness" and a marked "passion for seizing the ridiculous" predominated. In VF, however, "he does not use his weapons for the mere sake of caricature." Characters are fully developed and the "truth and energy" of the novel give it an interest which other writers must achieve with an intricate plot and over-wrought pathos.

*70.B *Times*, July 10, p. 8.
Review of VF. T's conciseness and refusal to attenuate, so marked in MPB, are still evident. Now, however, he has produced a "finished historical picture." He has not succumbed to the fallacy "that one isolated quality may . . . be made to look like a human being." T's pathos "reminds one of the exquisite touches which occur in . . . *Amelia*." He is rightly compared to Fielding because of the ability to detect motive

and the use of irony. VF is a faithful picture of the times it proposes to represent. True, "the tale is for the sake of the characters," but the interest is well enough sustained to satisfy readers who want an exciting story.

71.B [Forster, John]. *Examiner* (July 22), pp. 468-470.
VF is an "original work of real genius," and T falls short of Fielding only because of his lack of simple human affection, and the necessity he finds to sneer. Though characters are drawn from life and without exaggeration, there is a tendency to select the "grotesque and unpleasing lineaments," though, to be sure, "vice and folly are never made alluring."

*72.B [Rintoul, Robert S.]. *Spectator*, XXI (July 22), 709-710; Rptd. *Living Age*, XVIII (Aug. 26), 412-416.
VF is a "pungent, though good-natured satire," that "displays a depth, and at times a pathos," not found in previous work. "But it is rather a succession of connected scenes and characters, than a well-constructed story. . . . T seems to have looked at life by bits rather than as a whole." The heroines do not make up for the lack of a hero, "since one is without a heart, and the other is without a head"; though Becky, "as a creation or *character*," can hardly be matched in prose fiction. The "conclusion . . . is not only wrong as wanting in poetical justice, but untrue as a picture of society. . . ."

*73.B [Lewes, George H.]. *Athenaeum* (Aug. 12), pp. 794-797.
VF is "one of the most remarkable works of modern fiction." T's style is "winning, easy, masculine . . ." and he "indulges in no sentimentalities—inflicts no fine writing," but rather trusts "to the force of truth and humor." Characters are not vicious or virtuous in accordance with whether they are rich or poor. T is "unfettered by political or social theories." He describes "the latent absurdity grinning under a moral mask" by means of irony, but he "uses it far too exclusively." Other faults: the full range of human nature is slighted, in preference to vice and folly; "The passions are taken at their culminating point, not exhibited in the process of growth."

74.B "A Contrast." *Bentley's Miscellany*, XXIV (Sept.), 248-255.
VF, the work of "one of the most practical, plain speaking, and *nonchalant* novelists," is compared with a current romance. VF "promises to become a classic," though it in-

dulges in "the practice of morbid anatomy." T is taken to task for suggesting that Becky would do outright murder.

*75.B [Bell, Robert]. *Fraser's Magazine*, XXXVIII (Sept.), 320-333.
VF "is a novel without a plan," though its several narratives "frequently help each other on." "The real interest . . . [begins after] the marriage bells." T "dissects his victims with a smile," a trait that may be traced back to his earlier work. But "he cannot call up a tear without dashing it off with a sarcasm."

76.A *Knickerbocker*, XXXII (Sept.), 249-254.
Review of VF, praising its "acute observation and perception of the actions and motives of the English world," and remarking its "exquisite sense of the burlesque and the *bizarre.* . . ."

77.A *Sartain's Union Magazine*, III (Sept.), 144.
Review of Vol. I, VF (New York). It is "decidedly the best work of its author." T "has not the earnest pathos of . . . [Dickens]; but his style is more bold and compact." Though T would seem to desire "that the reader should be made 'sadder and wiser,' " VF is really productive of good humor, and is recommended "to all who are down in the mouth."

*78.A B[risted], C[harles] A. *American (Whig) Review*, VIII (Oct.), 421-431; Rptd. *Pieces of a Broken Down Critic*. 2 vols. Baden-Baden: Scotzniovsky, 1858, I, 195-215.
VF "is a book to keep and read, and there are many sermons in it." T "is greater as a moralist than as a humorist." The disagreeable characters are expressly presented to serve the "moral and end of the story." But T does not give due credit to "true Christian men and women."

79.B "Contemporary Authors—Mr. Thackeray." *Dublin University Magazine*, XXXII (Oct.), 444-459.
VF describes the effect fortune produces on each of the characters, "rather than any deep analysis of the passions or feelings of the human heart." T fails to do justice to the "generosity and self-devotion of a true woman." Equally distasteful is the implication that the real world "is so entirely peo-

pled with knaves and fools." In regard to Becky's end, T is thought to have shown self-control in not "heaping more retributive justice" upon her.

80.A *Godey's Lady's Book,* XXXVII (Oct.), 251.
Brief, cursory notice of VF. If book is without a hero, it "has heroines enough for twenty novels."

81.A *Holden's Dollar Magazine,* II (Oct.), 629-630.
VF is "a master-piece, *per se.*" "If he [T] resembles any romantic satirist, it is Cervantes." In all of his writings, he has but one motive—"to satirize the small vices of mankind."

*82.A [Whipple, Edwin P.]. "Novels of the Season." *North American Review,* LXVII (Oct.), 354-369; Rptd. *Essays and Reviews.* 2 vols. New York: Appleton, 1849.
Review of VF (pp. 368-369) along with novels by the Brontës, Bulwer, and others. The romances of this collection are given curt treatment, especially Bulwer's "affectation of philosophy and . . . affectation of noble sentiments." In contrast, VF "is an attempt to represent the world as it is." T "has Fielding's cosy manner of talking to his readers and, like Fielding, takes his personages mostly from ordinary life." Of all the authors reviewed, only T "preserves himself from the illusions of misanthropy or sentimentality, and though dealing with a host of selfish and malicious characters, his book leaves no impression that the world is past praying for."

83.A *United States Magazine & Democratic Review,* XXIII (Oct.), 377-379.
"VF is the embodiment of the Maxims of La Rochefoucault." T "is too cynical to indulge in the melting mood." Nevertheless, his technique is to lead "the reader with Sentiment on one arm and Satire on the other." The marriages, because they come at the beginning of the story, fail to preserve "the unity of action." Becky is an attractive character because "she is talented, energetic—and successful."

84.A *Graham's Magazine,* XXXIII (Nov.), 297.
VF "follows the track of Fielding rather than Bulwer, and aims at representing the world as it is." T's tone is far from being over-worldly or morbid. He is neither "the hater nor the sentimentalist."

85.A *Sartain's Union Magazine*, III (Nov.), 240.
Brief notice of Vol. II, VF (New York) repeats notion of
book's good-humor. (See No. 77 above.)

86.B [Hervey, Thomas K.]. *Athenaeum* (Nov. 4), pp. 1099-1101.
Notice of first no. of P. There is a reluctance to anticipate
the work because of the example of VF, which "contrived
to escape the foresight of the critics." In contrast to VF, P
begins well, and there is "a suggestion . . . of pre-conceived
design."

87.B [Rintoul, Robert S.]. *Spectator*, XXI (Nov. 4), 1070.
Brief notice of first no. of P. "Opens with greater promise
than did VF. . . . There is a greater breadth and largeness in
the kind of life to which we are introduced." Pen's "scrapes
and peccadilloes will not be so distasteful as those of Re-
becca," if only because he is a man.

88.B *Morning Chronicle*, Nov. 7, p. 3.
Good wishes extended to T on appearance of first no. of P,
which "promises to be in no degree inferior to its successful
predecessor."

*89.B Brontë, Charlotte. *Jane Eyre*. Preface, 2nd ed. 3 vols. London: Smith, Elder, I, x-xi.
T, to whom *Jane Eyre* is dedicated, is called "the first social
regenerator of the day." His "words are not framed to tickle
delicate ears; . . . and he speaks truth as deep, with a power
as prophet-like and as vital," as that of the son of Imlah before the kings of Judah and Israel.

*90.B "Humorists—Dickens and Thackeray." *English Review*, X
(Dec.), 257-275; Rptd. *Living Age*, XXI (May 5, 1849),
224-232; *Eclectic Magazine*, XVI (March, 1849), 370-379.
Review of VF and *Dombey and Son*. A distinction is drawn
between wit and humor, noting that the latter is compatible
with the Christian spirit. Dickens and T are "suns of humor"
who cause other writers to "pale and dim." But Dickens has
shown a "tendency to vague and pernicious sentimentalism,"
in spite of his virtues, e.g., his excellent portrayal of children,
his strong sense of locality. However, "T is a far more powerful moralist . . . ; he understands grown men and women
better," and in his work "nothing is forced, nothing artificial."

*91.B [Rigby, Elizabeth]. *Quarterly Review*, LXXXIV (Dec.), 153-185; Rptd. *Living Age*, XX (March 17, 1849), 497-511; *Famous Reviews*, ed. R. B. Johnson. London, 1914.
Review of VF and *Jane Eyre*. No attempt is made at comparison or joint discussion of the two. It is merely that both are exceptional and "do not fit any ready-made criticism." VF is more of a history of average sufferings and pleasures than it is a novel with a contrived plot. Good humor, tact, and self-possession are the things with which Becky charms us; and she and Rawdon do, in fact, love each other in a way. T's hint that she should be a murderess is improbable. Overall, VF provides "a literal photograph of the manners and habits of the 19th century."

92.A *Literary World*, III (Dec. 9), 896.
Review of GHD (New York). Praise of T and his great achievement, VF, prefaces the comment that in GHD are "several passages of touching appeal, worthy of being bound up with Fielding's *Amelia*."

93.B *Literary Gazette*, XXXII (Dec. 23), 835-836.
Extracts of DB favorably presented, but without direct critical comment.

94.B *Spectator*, XXI (Dec. 23), 1236-1237.
DB equals if it does not excel MPB or OS. T has the gift of brevity, "and very often a single sentence brings a world of character before the mind."

95.B *Athenaeum* (Dec. 30), p. 1322.
DB, though a trifle, shows the work of "a master-hand," and is "not without its morals."

96.B *Britannia*, IX (Dec. 30), 843.
Review of DB. "The texture of the book is slight, but the threads are of genuine quality. The author of VF is recognizable in every line." But the drawings carry the burlesque too far.

97.B *John Bull*, XXVIII (Dec. 30), 839.
Brief notice of DB, commending it as a "seasonable holiday gift," and noting that its portrayals are "but too true to life."

1849

98.B *New Monthly Magazine*, LXXXV (Jan.), 141.
Brief notice of DB. "When dealing with youth, T is humorous without ill-nature."

99.A *Literary World*, IV (Jan. 6), 9-11.
Excerpts of first no. of P (London) with an introductory word of praise.

100.A *Godey's Lady's Book*, XXXVIII (Feb.), 152.
Brief notice of GHD. "One scene . . . surpasses in beauty and pathos anything . . . by Dickens."

101.A *Graham's Magazine*, XXXIV (Feb.), 152.
GHD cannot compare with VF.

102.A *Holden's Dollar Magazine*, III (Feb.), 113.
Brief notice of GHD, expressing pleasure at T's growing popularity in the United States.

103.B *Athenaeum* (Feb. 10), pp. 137-138.
GHD reflects "its family likeness to VF." Similarly, MW. T is requested to produce in the future "characters of a more agreeable quality."

104.B *Literary Gazette*, XXXIII (March 17), 190.
GHD should have been more popular when first appearing in *Fraser's*. In that class of periodical writing it "was a Mountain of Light."

105.A *Sartain's Union Magazine*, IV (April), 288.
Brief notice of GHD. It is amusing, though "we cannot . . . admire his style as much as some . . . critics do."

106.B *Rambler*, IV (May), 48-51.
Review of Nos. 1-6 of P. "This will be the best of T's stories" —"as clever as VF, and far more agreeable." "T's tendency to overdraw . . . his characters is . . . more restrained. . . ." There is also "less of the writer's affectation of perpetually introducing himself to the attention of the reader."

107.A Chasles, Philarete. "A Personal Sketch of Thackeray." *Literary World*, IV (June 23), 530-531; Trans. from Chasles's "Le Roman de Moeurs en Angleterre." *Revue des Deux Mondes*, 6th ser. I (Feb. 15, 1849), 537-571.
Only the first few pages of the original Chasles article are used. The biographical information, as presented, makes T appear a very fast and rakish young fellow. YP, C, GHD, ISB, S, and his early magazine work are credited to T.

108.A *Literary World*, V (Aug. 25), 154-155.
Review of first no. of P (New York). The "lighter vein" of P does not promise to "maintain the stamina of VF." T's strength is in "satirical pictures of a purely worldly life."

109.B [Croker, John W.]. "Tours in Ireland." *Quarterly Review*, LXXXV (Sept.), 491-562.
ISB discussed along with other books on Ireland. Beneath its "merriment and *persiflage,* a great deal of sober, useful truth" is to be found in ISB. "The picture presented is striking and true, and the hints as to the causes of misery there are judicious."

110.A *Godey's Lady's Book*, XXXIX (Oct.), 293-294.
Brief notice of first no. of P (New York) refrains from making premature judgment.

111.A *Holden's Dollar Magazine*, IV (Oct.), 636.
Notice of first no. of P (New York). "In no respect inferior to any of his other works."

112.A *Southern Literary Messenger*, XV (Nov.), 699-701.
Review of third no. of P (New York). P is an improvement over other writings, and "contains some more lenient readings of human motives than [VF]." Compared to the Gothic novels and the novels of doctrine, T's work is far superior. T exposes foibles in terms as unmistakable as Bunyan's. He is genial rather than cynical; and "his terror of maudlin sentiment," which makes him cover pathetic passages with irony, is the very thing "that renders his pathos so exquisite."

113.A *United States Magazine and Democratic Review*, XXV (Nov.), 478.
Brief notice of first three nos. of P (New York). "T sur-

passes most of the other London novel writers, not excepting Dickens."

114.B "Christmas Books." *Athenaeum* (Dec. 29), pp. 1329-1330.
Review of Reb. "Such a harlequinade . . . has not been thrown off since Hood laid by pen and pun."

115.B *John Bull*, XXIX (Dec. 29), 823.
Reb is too long to sustain its facetious tone.

116.B *Spectator*, XXII (Dec. 29), 1236-1237; Rptd. *Living Age*, XXIV (March 2, 1850), 385-387.
Reb is eminently appropriate as a Christmas book, providing also a good "satire upon the conventionally perverted views of history."

1850

117.B *Morning Chronicle*, Jan. 3, p. 4.
Editorial states that T unconsciously fosters "baneful prejudice" against literary men by his depiction of the literary life in P. [T's reply printed Jan. 12, p. 4. (T's *Letters*, ed. G. N. Ray, II, 629.) See Nos. 118, 119, and 124 below.]

118.B [Forster, John]. "Encouragement of Literature by the State." *Examiner* (Jan. 5), p. 2.
T is criticized for disparaging the literary profession in P. (See No. 117 above and No. 119 below.)

119.B [Forster, John]. "The Dignity of Literature." *Examiner* (Jan. 19), p. 35.
Reply to T's rebuttal to Nos. 117 and 118 above.

120.A *Literary World*, VI (Feb. 16), 151-152.
Review of No. 4 of P (New York). T's style "rarely . . . sounds the depths of nature, and it has not the dramatic power of Dickens, but within its privileged range of manners, . . . it is supreme. No man can handle a conventionalism with the insight and coolness of T."

121.B "The Age of Chivalry—Mr. Thackeray!" *Freeman's Journal* (Dublin), April 8, Fol. 2.

T is hotly criticized for "his unmanly grossness" in referring to Catherine Hayes (the Irish opera singer) as a murderess in No. 15 of P. [Actually T's allusion is to a convicted criminal of the same name.]

122.A *American (Whig) Review*, XII (July), 3.

Brief notice of first half of P (New York), superficially praising it.

123.A *Southern Quarterly Review*, XVII (July), 538.

Brief notice of No. 4 of P (New York). "The life and interest continue to be sustained with all the spirit of T."

124.B [Masson, David]. "Pendennis—The Literary Profession." *North British Review*, XIII (Aug.), 335-372; Rptd. *Eclectic Magazine*, XXI (Nov.), 364-380.

A polemic in defense of T's portrayal of literary men in P. T's picture is disagreeable in parts, but it is not essentially untrue. He merely puts literary men on an equal footing with other men, rather than exalting them. (See Nos. 117, 118, and 119 above.)

125.A *Sartain's Union Magazine*, VII (Aug.), 124.

Brief notice of No. 5 of P (New York), noting that it is "generally pronounced superior to VF."

126.A *Literary World*, VII (Aug. 3), 93.

Review of *Stubbs's Calendar* (New York). "We hope to see it followed by the other less known tales of the author."

127.A *Knickerbocker*, XXXVI (Sept.), 277-278.

Review of *Stubbs's Calendar* (New York). More valuable than the amusement, which T seems always able to provide, "is the moral lesson conveyed by the history."

128.B Frank, Parson. "William Makepeace Thackeray." *People's & Howitt's Journal*, X, 217-220; Rptd. *Eclectic Magazine*, XXII (Jan. 1851), 80-85.

General critique of T's work through P, restating many of the opinions presented elsewhere: T's realism, his concern

for social reform, and his superiority over Dickens in describing "upper and middle life." T is defended from the charge
of cynicism by pointing out "those frequent bits of pathos"
in his work.

129.A *Holden's Dollar Magazine*, VI (Dec.), 758.
Brief notice of No. 6 of P (New York). The description of
bachelor life "is excruciatingly true to nature."

130.B *Daily News*, Dec. 2, p. 2.
Review of P along with *David Copperfield*. Both are "woven
. . . out of the common stuff of English life." T avoids "the
transcendental or preternatural. He is a puritan in his rejec-
tion of ornament." P's forte is its women, who "shine as
bright as the most ideal fancy could make them." The serial
form is criticized for tending to destroy dramatic unity.

131.B [Chorley, Henry F.]. *Athenaeum* (Dec. 7), pp. 1273-1275.
P "cannot be described as an advance on VF." T is still "an
admirable writer of clear, succinct, vigorous English" but
why must he "be always 'going to the fair'?"

132.B [Findlay, John R.]. *Scotsman*, XXXIV, Dec. 18, Fol. 3.
P is worthy of VF. By necessity, T's manner and views repeat themselves, "but there are here a greater variety both of
character and sentiment, and a less constant indulgence in
that cynical philosophy. . . . He remonstrates as a brother,
rather than reproves as a judge. . . . As a . . . moral anato-
mist, T is . . . without a peer."

133.B *Athenaeum* (Dec. 21), pp. 1340-1341.
K "is a lively *ephemeron*: meant by its shrewd author for
nothing better."

*134.B [Lewes, George H.]. *Leader,* I (Dec. 21), 929-930.
Review of P. "England has at no time produced a writer of
fiction with whom T may not stand in honorable comparison."
His reputation will rest on his truth and his style, which has
"clearness, strength, idiomatic ease, delicacy, and variety."
Not merely concerned with the surface of things, he sees society "and sees through it." It is "a predominating tendency
to *antithesis*" which accounts for T's debunking, rather than
merely a "mocking spirit." In P there is a "decided advance

upon VF with respect to a . . . more generous view of humanity."

135.B [Rintoul, Robert S.]. "Thackeray's *Pendennis.*" *Spectator,* XXIII, Dec. 21), 1213-1215.
P is designed to please those who enjoy "sketches of themselves in all the attitudes of real life, drawn with a vigour and truth seldom equalled." However, T does not "frame a coherent story . . . , illustrate any speculative theory of life, . . . or embody in his fictions the great social questions of the day." His work does have a moral purpose though, and can be considered "as a protest against this corruption of the individual by society."

136.B *Spectator,* XXIII (Dec. 21), 1217.
K exhibits T's "knowledge of society, and his shrewdness of remark, as well as his pleasant style; but it is not the happiest of his effusions."

137.B *Literary Gazette,* XXXIV (Dec. 28), 961-962.
K is "unhealthy in its tone," in spite of humor and inimitable sketches. The "over-bending of little foibles" is not properly a part of the Christmas spirit.

1851

Entries for this year are arranged chronologically, as usual, with the exception that the notices of T's lectures in London are grouped together following other entries.

138.B "A Gossip About Christmas Books." *Fraser's Magazine,* XLIII (Jan.), 37-46.
K does not provide enough "novelty in the way of character." T should recognize "the more healthy qualities of head and heart."

*139.B "W. M. Thackeray & Arthur Pendennis, Esquires." *Fraser's Magazine,* XLIII (Jan.), 75-90.
T's characters "only play at passion." "When he does depict a whole-hearted passion . . . he makes us feel that it is ridiculous in its excess." T was applauded for VF by the "stalls

and boxes," whereas "the pit is the most enthusiastic" for Dickens. And "T can only be thoroughly appreciated . . . by the small class who are familiar with . . . the society he describes." In P, "moral interest should have centered in . . . [Pen], but it does not." Fortunately, T didn't try "drawing a MAN," since no book should be written that a father cannot permit his daughter to read.

140.A "The Genius and Writings of Thackeray." *Southern Quarterly Review*, XIX (Jan.), 74-100.
GHD, P, and primarily VF serve as the basis for comments. T's truthful picture of men and manners is contrasted to the contrived plots and pathos-ridden works of others. He describes life "as he himself has seen it, and not as it is learned from the experience of others." T only "uses story as a means, and not as an end." His real interest is to examine the groundwork of society and men's motives.

141.B [Kenney, Charles L.]. *Times*, Jan. 3, p. 6; Rptd. *Literary World*, VIII (Feb. 8), 111-113; *Living Age*, XXVIII (March 8), 473-475.
Review of K which prompted T's preface to 2nd ed. K suggests "the rinsings of a void brain." Since "he cannot draw his men and women with their skins off," the drawings "are pleasanter . . . than the flayed anatomies of the letter-press." (See No. 144 below.)

142.A *Literary World*, VIII (Jan. 18), 45-46.
Review of P (New York). T's work compliments the reader's own common sense. It conveys "the self-contained enthusiasm of a man subdued yet strengthened by experience." But because "the heart gets but the beggar's pittance," T will be less popular than Dickens. P seems to duplicate many characters of VF in new dress. This, however, does not seem a failing.

143.A "The Author of *Pendennis* Reviewing His Reviewer." *Literary World*, VIII (Feb. 8), 111-113; Rptd. *Living Age*, XXVIII (March 8), 473-475.
T's preface to 2nd ed. of K (London), in which he replies to No. 141 above, is cited as an "exhibition of literary fencing" that will provide "the most piquant literary entertain-

ment of the day." T 's preface (inclusive of No. 141) is reprinted in lieu of a review of K.

144.A *North American Miscellany*, I (Feb. 15), 143-144.
The *Times*'s harsh treatment of K (No. 141 above) is pro-
tested. But T's reply "showed equally bad taste." "When
he has need to argue for his cleverness, his cleverness can
hardly be very apparent."

145.B *Bentley's Miscellany*, XXIX (March), 342.
Review of K. Satire does not lend itself to the making of a
good Christmas book.

146.A [Simms, William G.]. "Critical Notices." *Southern Quarterly
Review*, XIX (April), 559.
P is a "close and satirical delineation of human life in its ordinary conditions," and "perhaps among the best" of T's writings. But, "in truth, his art is not of the highest character."

147.A "Pendennis and His Contemporaries." *American (Whig) Review*, XIII (May), 395-398.
Realism is the final criterion of a good novelist, and, therefore, T stands above Bulwer and Dickens. In P the characters
"neither sentimentalize about love, nor talk Platonic meta-
physics at one another. . . . They are natural without being
commonplace."

*148.B [Masson, David]. "Pendennis & Copperfield: Thackeray &
Dickens." *North British Review*, XV (May), 57-89; Rptd.
Living Age, XXX (July 19), 97-110; extracts rptd. *International Magazine*, III (July 1), 532-533; The *Age* (Richmond,
Va.), I (March), 227-229.
"T and Dickens, Dickens and T—the two names now almost
necessarily go together." But "no two writers are so dissimilar." Just as in painting there are the schools of the real and
the ideal, so too in writing. They involve different approaches
and do not imply a condemnation of each other. All aspects
of these men's work follow the basic difference. In style, T
is "more terse and idiomatic"; Dickens, "more diffuse and
luxuriant." The latter does not create life-like characters, but
fastens on to one trait and takes it off to an ideal region. He
is free, though, to embrace a wider range, whereas T is "more
restricted" by adhering to the real.

*149.B "David Copperfield, and Pendennis." *Prospective Review*, VII (May), 157-191.
Serial writing detracts from art (i.e., form). Dickens overcomes the difficulty to a greater degree. Both use a "panoramic style of writing," in which "numberless characters pass before the eye, and numberless openings through which glimpses of their lives are discerned. . . ." T repudiates sentimentality on the one hand, but at the same time looks at life from "the point of view of an effeminate sentimentalist of two-and-twenty. He is always disheartened and aimless." Dickens' view, therefore, is healthier.

150.A "Thackeray and Dickens." *Literary World*, VIII (June 7), 455-457.
T's place is acknowledged alongside "the most popular of living English writers." (Extensive quotations are provided from No. 148 above.)

*151.B [Phillips, Samuel]. "David Copperfield and Arthur Pendennis." *Times*, June 11, p. 8; Rptd. *Southern Literary Messenger*, XVII (Aug.), 499-504; *London Times Essays*. 2nd series. London, 1852.
P is less exciting. Its real merit consists in its truth of representation. The biographical form of *Copperfield* provided it with "an additional reality" and thus a special interest. The real and artificial (ideal) approaches are distinguished (following the lead of No. 148 above), and each of the authors is seen as possessing special virtues and liabilities. *Copperfield* is finally preferred because in it "the most universal interest is conciliated and the most exalted teaching hidden beneath the tale."

152.A [Griswold, Rufus W.]. *International Magazine*, III (July 1), 464-465.
Extracts from London notices of first two EH lectures are prefaced by the information that T will come to the U. S., and will probably write something about it afterwards.

153.A [Griswold, Rufus W.]. "The British Humorists: Described by Mr. Thackeray." *International Magazine* IV (Aug.), 24-26.
Extracts from London notices of last four EH lectures, to which is added some critical comment: "Mr. T is not a

humorist . . . ; he is a cold satirist, sneering at humanity."
K is "but unredeemable vulgarity." T himself is the epitome
of "the snob cynical and supercilious."

154.B *Dublin University Magazine*, XXXVIII (Aug.), 193-206.
Review of P. T's writings are not truly novels. They lack
plot and "scenes of highly wrought interest." Pen is a com-
posite of "the failings and weaknesses" of his class, and is
thus an unattractive and poorly executed character. T is also
upbraided for anti-Irish sentiments, evidenced by his portrayal of Costigan.

Notices of EH Lectures

(Only those are listed which make comments beyond reporting the text of the lecture.)

155.B "Mr. Thackeray's Lectures." *Daily News*, May 23, p. 5.
First lecture showed T to have "philosophical insight, with a
kindred genius, and [was presented] in the natural, lively,
social, and life-like way which might be expected from the
author of P and VF."

156.B "Mr. Thackeray's Lectures." *Morning Chronicle*, May 23,
p. 5.
First lecture: T, who has redeemed present-day fiction, is
the man best fitted to deliver these lectures. Swift is a kindred subject to an uncompromising satirist like T. The overall treatment is essentially philosophic.

157.B. "Mr. Thackeray's Lectures." *Morning Post*, May 23, p. 5.
First lecture: "His style is exceedingly elegant, and his meta-
phors happy and suitable; but the assertions and principles
they convey are by no means to be implicitly followed."

158.B "Mr. Thackeray's Lectures." *Times*, May 23, p. 6.
First lecture is as much a "critical dissertation" as it is "a
biography." T is no idolater. "Audience was numerous and
of the most select kind."

159.B [Forster, John]. "Mr. Thackeray's Lectures." *Examiner*
(May 24), pp. 325-326; Rptd. *Eclectic Magazine*, XXIII
(Aug.), 554-555.
First lecture: Swift was not fully or properly judged by T,
who made him appear too black or white in turn.

160.B *Leader*, II (May 24), 489.
First lecture: "The Fielding of our times" delivered a lecture
that was "thoughtful and picturesque."

161.B [Hunt, Leigh]. "Mr. Thackeray's Lectures." *Spectator*, XXIV
(May 24), 493-494; Rptd. *Living Age*, XXX (July 5), 11-
12.
T's examination proceeds from "sympathy not malignity,"
just as he satirizes with "gentleness and tenderness." The
lectures "are like conversation, like his books, like himself."

162.B "Mr. Thackeray's Second Lecture." *Daily News*, May 30,
p. 4.
"Even more than the last . . . a delightful specimen of the
author's power."

163.B "Mr. Thackeray's Lectures." *Morning Chronicle*, May 30,
p. 7.
Second lecture: This and the first are "charming and intellectual essays." Nevertheless, T, "having underrated Congreve, proceeded to overrate Addison."

164.B "Mr. Thackeray's Lectures." *Morning Post*, May 30, p. 5.
Second lecture: "Favouritism is . . . the great fault of these
lectures." T describes the facts of Congreve's and Addison's
lives but "the why and wherefore he leaves entirely alone."
No new ideas about the men or their times were presented.

165.B "Mr. Thackeray's Lectures." *Times*, May 30, p. 8.
Second lecture: Larger audience than the first. T's delivery
louder and clearer.

166.B [Forster, John]. "Mr. Thackeray's Second Lecture." *Ex-
aminer* (May 31), pp. 342-343; Rptd. *Living Age*, XXX
(July 19), 135-136.
T "violently underrated Congreve and as violently overrated
Addison."

167.B *Leader*, II (May 31), 515.
Second lecture: The part about Congreve was "full of exquisite touches. . . . But the . . . part . . . relating to Addison
was less graphic, less true, less interesting." There was an
"excessive overrating of Addison."

168.B "Mr. Thackeray's Lectures." *Daily News*, June 13, p. 5.
Third lecture: "Perhaps the most philosophical he has yet
delivered."

169.B "Mr. Thackeray's Lectures." *Times*, June 13, p. 6.
Third lecture "attracted even a larger audience."

170.B [Forster, John]. "Mr. Thackeray's Third Lecture." *Examiner*
(June 14), pp. 374-375; Rptd. *Living Age*, XXX (Aug. 2),
237-238.
Apology is tendered for having questioned T's accuracy re
Congreve in No. 166 above. Third lecture served as "a most
delightful and genial tribute" to Steele.

171.B *Leader*, II (June 14), 560.
Third lecture was remarkable more as a picture of the wit
and manners of the eighteenth century than as a study of
Steele.

172.B "Mr. Thackeray's Lectures." *Daily News*, June 20, p. 5.
Fourth lecture: Prior and Gay were "portrayed and discussed
—in a way at once so simple and so graphic."

173.B "Mr. Thackeray's Lectures." *Morning Post*, June 20, p. 5.
Third and fourth lectures: Regarding Steele, "we can hardly
justify the lecturer in occupying so refined an audience with
a number of threadbare details, which any student . . . would
be reproached for not knowing." The comments on Prior,
Gay, and Pope were "the veriest trifling." T will not enhance
his reputation by making the great names of literature "the
medium for trite observation."

174.B *Leader*, II (June 21), 586.
Fourth lecture was "fuller . . . of matter without losing anything in brilliancy of manner."

175.B "Mr. Thackeray's Lectures." *Daily News,* June 27, p. 5;
Rptd. *Examiner* (June 28), pp. 406-407.
Fifth lecture: "It is a matter for curious observation that T
should have spoken less charitably of *Tom Jones,* than both
Coleridge and Lamb have done."

176.B "Mr. Thackeray's Lectures." *Morning Chronicle,* June 27,
p. 5; Rptd. *Living Age,* XXX (Aug. 16), 334-335.
Fifth lecture: T is "in advance of his age" for remarking that
he was glad to see that the "gallows-lesson" was a practice no
longer in favor.

177.B "Mr. Thackeray's Lectures." *Morning Post,* June 27, p. 5.
Fifth lecture reported grudgingly, with the comment that it
yields even less than the previous ones. It is "*jejune* and
trifling," and completely barren. "Mr. T has greatly underrated the intelligence and perception of his audience."

178.B *Leader,* II (June 28), 610.
Fifth lecture: Less interesting than those previous. T's opinions "we constantly find open to question; but it is not as a
Course of Criticism that these Lectures have their inexpres-
sible charm."

179.B "Mr. Thackeray's Lectures." *Daily News,* July 4, p. 5; Rptd.
Living Age, XXX (Aug. 30), 399-400.
Sixth lecture: "There was marked sympathy in the applause
which greeted his discourse."

180.B "Mr. Thackery's Lectures." *Morning Chronicle,* July 4, p. 5.
Sixth lecture "terminated a course of as intellectual and pleasant lectures as we have ever had the gratification of hearing."

181.B "Mr. Thackeray's Lectures." *Morning Post,* July 4, p. 5.
Sixth lecture "was more vigorous, earnest, and pointed than
any . . . yet delivered." T's denunciation of Sterne's "sickly
sensibility" is commended in a qualified way.

182.B [Forster, John]. "Mr. Thackeray's Last Lecture." *Examiner*
(July 5), 422.
"The treatment of Sterne was . . . a piece of extravagant injustice," nor did Goldsmith fare much better "under the
superabundance of pitying praise poured out upon him."

1852

Entries for this year are arranged chronologically, as usual, with the exception that the notices of T's lectures in the United States are grouped together following other entries.

183.A *Graham's Magazine*, XL (Jan.), 112.
One paragraph notice of *Sketches of Ireland* (Phila., n.d.), which is probably a pirated ISB. It "abounds with the finest touches of the author's satirical pencil."

184.A *Literary World*, X (March 27), 220-221.
YP (New York) foreshadows VF and P, but its satire is harsher.

185.A G[reenwood], G[race]. [pseud. of Sara J. Lippincott]. *National Era* (Washington, D. C.), VI, Apr. 15, p. 63.
Brief notice of YP (New York). T's writing has the rare combination of "mellow humor with sharp satire," and YP is a perfect antidote for "the nervous prostration produced by some of the high wrought romances of the day."

186.A [Ellis, George E.]. *Christian Examiner*, LII (May), 456-457.
Review of YP (New York). "Though there is a painful and revolting story involved in it, if it be rightly interpreted it will be a solemn monitor."

187.A *Literary World*, X (May 1), 307-308.
Review of PSB (New York). General approval of the sketches, as well as T's bits of philosophy.

188.A *American (Whig) Review*, XV (June), 564.
Brief notice of PSB (New York), without pertinent comment on the book. Instead, general praise of T's truthfulness and satire is given.

189.A *Graham's Magazine*, XL (June), 665.
Brief notice of YP (New York). "The spelling alone is a work of genius."

190.A *Graham's Magazine*, XLI (July), 107.
Brief notice of PSB (New York). T's "English sense . . . is
somewhat too constantly accompanied by his English prejudice; but even where he loses his fairness he never loses his
brilliancy."

191.A *Literary World*, XI (Aug. 28), 134-135.
Review of S (New York). T lashes abuses, but "nature and
truth . . . come off triumphantly."

192.A [Bennett, James G.]. "Another Cockney Character Coming
Over." New York *Herald*, Sept. 18, Fol. 4.
The literary toadyism of New Yorkers is scoffed at, especially
that of the "old womanish societies" who have engaged T to
come and lecture. Possibly defensible if the fanfare were for
Macaulay, Bulwer, Dickens, or even James, "it is ridiculous"
for a "literary snob" like T.

193.A *Graham's Magazine*, XLI (Oct.), 445.
Brief notice of S (New York). S contains the philosophy
which VF and P illustrate.

194.A *Knickerbocker*, XL (Oct.), 350.
Review of S (New York). It is fortunate that "this very
picture of English 'snobbery'. . . should have been written
by one of their own countrymen; a man, moreover, of rare
accomplishments."

195.A "Thackeray." *Southern Literary Messenger*, XVIII (Oct.),
611.
VF is clearly "a more powerful work than P" which is diffuse
and sketchy despite many well-drawn characters. "As a satirist T ranks with the very first writers." His work gives one
"the impression that English society is rotten to the core."

196.A [Simms, William G.]. "Critical Notices." *Southern Quarterly
Review*, XXII (Oct.), 545.
Brief notice of S (New York) admits not having read book,
but offers some general praise of T.

197.A *Literary World*, XI (Oct. 23), 265.
MW (New York) is less elaborate, and "far less genial" than
T's later work. "He does not gild and sentimentalize over
vice."

198.B [Maddyn, D. Owen]. *Athenaeum* (Nov. 6), pp. 1199-1201.
E shows "wide display of mastery over the rhetoric of fiction.
. . . But no fresh fount of thought is touched." Nor are there
truly new characters. The hero's life is "unnatural—at the
least, extremely improbable." The ending is both disappointing and questionable. His marriage with Rachel "affects us
somewhat like a marriage with his own mother."

199.B [Lewes, George H.]. "Thackeray's New Novel." *Leader*, III
(Nov. 6), 1071-1072; Rptd. *Harper's Magazine*, VI (Jan.
1853), 210-212.
E "is a beautiful book," unlike VF or P. "The mocking
spirit has fled; such sarcasm as remains is of another sort—a
kind of sad smile, that speaks of pity, not scorn." It shows
"an advancing growth, both as a moralist and as an artist."
Defects of carelessness have been eliminated. "All who have
lived will feel here the pulse of real suffering, so different from
'romantic woe'; all who have loved will trace a real affection
here."

200.B *Literary Gazette*, XXXVI (Nov. 6), 823-825; (Nov. 13),
839-840.
E is disappointing as an historical novel. The transfer of affection from Beatrix to Rachel is questionable, and Henry's
marriage to the latter "is painful and almost shocking." Rachel
is a failure in much the same way that T's other good heroines
(Amelia, Helen, Laura) are. T's "half-sad, half-sardonic
vein of moralizing" mars the style and tone. In general, E
"can hardly raise the fame of one who has to be tried by the
high standard of VF."

*201.B [Brimley, George]. "Thackeray's *Esmond*." *Spectator*, XXV
(Nov. 6), 1066-1067; Rptd. *Harper's Magazine*, VI (Jan.
1853), 207-210; *Essays*. Cambridge: Macmillan, 1858, pp.
258-269.
E is historical in its devices and setting, but the main object
is the history of a family. "There is abundance of incident
. . . , but not much more plot than in one of Defoe's novels."
T's satire in VF arose from "the moral antithesis of actual
and ideal." In E, "the ideal is no longer implied, but realized." Esmond's life "is a record of his attachment to one
woman," towards whom an initially simple and childish affection grows into a complex feeling. T's great skill saves

the relation between them from becoming ridiculous or offensive. "The book is more of a complete whole" than VF or P, though perhaps "its excellences will not help it to a very large public."

202.B *Reynolds' Newspaper*, Nov. 7, p. 2.
E is free from "sly sarcasm or humorous portraiture of characters." "The subtle genius of T is yet fresh, vigorous, and racy," whereas Dickens is "struggling painfully and ineffectually against premature exhaustion."

203.A G., P. "A Sketch of Thackeray." New York *Evening Post*, Nov. 12, Fol. 2.
Information about T's career and his writings. VF is his great work though P is "a more interesting and consecutive narrative and breathes a deeper and more earnest tone of criticism." T is "made of sterner stuff" than Dickens. Neither jolly nor ideal, "he describes men as he has found them. . . . It is . . . not the individual he exposes but the social medium in which he has lived."

204.B [Forster, John]. *Examiner* (Nov. 13), pp. 723-726.
E, "by no means equal to VF in interest, excels even that . . . work as a display of literary power." The style is excellent, and "there is no excess, no strain after effect." But T is still deficient in feeling, and this is responsible for a lack of vitality in the characters. T stands over them not among them, either as God or a puppeteer. Rachel's steadfast love for Henry over the many years seems wholly incredible. This and other "ill-chosen material" seemingly waste T's genius and labor.

205.A [James, Henry]. "Thackeray." New York Daily *Tribune*, Nov. 13, p. 4.
A welcome to New York for "the most thoughtful critic of manners and society, the subtlest humorist, and the most effective, because the most genial, satirist the age has known." "Dickens—who is often absurdly compared to T"—has catered to the sentiment of a "romantic public," whereas T's characters "are stamped with nature's own signet."

206.A "Thackeray's New Work." New York *Times,* Nov. 19, p. 2.
Review of E. "In point of style and skill in composition, E is fully equal to its predecessors. The archaisms . . . are ex-

quisitely managed." And "the passages of moral reflection" are likewise equal to those in VF and P.

207.A [Young, William]. *Albion* (New York), N.S. XI, Nov. 20, 559-560.
T is received in New York "with more dignity and self-respect than awaited [Dickens]," and this reflects their differences as authors. Dickens seems "created for stage effect," just as his "grotesque and exaggerated characters" are.

208.A "Mr. Thackeray's New Novel." New York *Evening Post*, Nov. 20, Fol. 1.
E (London) reached New York on Nov 18. British reviews of it (e.g., No. 199 above) are quoted.

209.B *Weekly Dispatch*, Nov. 21, p. 742.
E is "another proof that . . . [T is] one of the most original, vigorous, and masculine minds." Though his writing is "generally accepted as of the cynical order," he "has as much malice in his sound, healthy heart as a new born babe."

210.A "Mr. Thackeray's *Henry Esmond*." *Literary World*, XI (Nov. 29), 339-340.
The historical technique of E lies between the antiquarianism of Bulwer and the modernizations of Scott. The contemporary satirist, however, slyly lurks behind the narration; and other touches (e.g., the opening scenes with the child, Henry) reflect nineteenth-century attitudes.

211.B "*Esmond* and *Basil*." *Bentley's Miscellany*, XXXII (Dec.), 576-586.
E cannot be placed "in the front rank of historical novels. . . . The romance derives little aid from the history." "The great beauty of E . . . lies in the portraiture of Rachel." The story of her domestic affairs is an old one, though never told "with more delicate truthfulness." E can take its place alongside VF and P.

*212.B "Mr. Thackeray's *Esmond*." *Fraser's Magazine*, XLVI (Dec.), 622-633.
"The predominance . . . of analysis and description over the dramatic element" will disappoint certain readers. But "there is higher literary power and kindlier and truer humanity in

this work" than in any of T's other books. "The story is more like a family chronicle than a novel." T, however, misreads human nature when he describes the failure of the Castlewood marriage. Lady Castlewood "exhibits a mixture of incongruities that contradicts all experience" (e.g., mourning for her husband while cherishing a love for Harry). And in the end, instead of strength and purity, "we find nothing but . . . the mere dross of pent up passion."

213.A *Graham's Magazine*, XLI (Dec.), 664.
Brief notice of MW (New York), which finds satire, caricature, and hearty humor the prime ingredients of these "articles."

214.B *Irish Quarterly Review*, II (Dec.), 849-870.
Review of E. Both the manner of narration (the changing personal pronouns) and the complicated chronology tend to confusion. Also, T's attempt to make history "familiar" rather than "heroic" does not succeed. The use of the language of a past age, however, is successful, except for T's interruptions *"in propria persona."* E will be appreciated by "the literary antiquarian."

215.A *Knickerbocker*, XL (Dec.), 526-527.
Review of E (New York). *Times* review of Nov. 19 (No. 206 above) is reprinted, with added comment that T's presence will surely add to the popularity of the work.

216.B [Ainsworth, William H.]. *New Monthly Magazine*, XCVI (Dec.), 483-496.
Review of E. "In spite of a meagre plot with an unsatisfactory éclaircissement . . ., he has contrived to interest us in his story." This is due mainly to the manner in which it is written. T's tendency to view the worst side of human nature persists, and here he has gone so far as to blacken historical personalities and manipulate history to his own ends.

217.B *Sharpe's London Magazine*, XVI (Dec.), 380-381.
Review of E that dwells more on T's general qualities; e.g., his close observation of motive, his "tenderness towards foolish women." "He would be a *great teacher* were he not so at war with small faults." Esmond is an ideal hero, and re-

garding his marriage to an older woman, "the 'Marrying Man' will at once agree in the wisdom of his choice."

218.A *Southern Literary Messenger*, XVIII (Dec.), 758-761.
E is "not so much a novel as a history of the age of Queen Anne." The dry bones of the historical personages are made to come alive. But E is still T the satirist, debunking that period as he has the present age. The character of Rachel should redeem T to those who said he "abused the sex."

219.A "Mr. Thackeray's Lectures Illustrated by *Henry Esmond.*" *Literary World*, XI (Dec. 18), 389-390.
The EH lectures and E complement each other.

220.A "The Lecture Season." New York *Recorder*, VII (Dec. 22) 154; Rptd. *Living Age*, XXXVI (March 5, 1853), 433-434.
T's EH lectures (though in good taste themselves) give new publicity to "some of the most objectionable writers in all English literature," some of whose novels are filled with "unmitigated filth and grossness." (See Nos. 243, 244, 245, 249 below.)

*221.B [Phillips, Samuel]. "Mr. Thackeray's New Novel." *Times*, Dec. 22, p. 8; Rptd. *Living Age*, XXXVI (Feb. 5, 1853), 277-280.
Review of E. T, whose strength is his own natural style and his ability to depict the current age, "suicidally determined" to write of the eighteenth century. In spite of literary devices, E is not a "representation of the spirit and soul of the time." It is a sham curiosity. Esmond's marriage to his own "dear Mother!" leaves us with a sentiment of "unaffected disgust." The true basis of T's fault, in E as in VF and P, is his view of life—"life looked upon with a disbelieving, a disappointed and a jaundiced eye. . . . Real, but only as sickness is real."

Notices of EH Lectures

(Only those are listed which make comments beyond reporting the text of the lecture.)

222.A [Bryant, William C.]. "Mr. Thackeray's Lecture." New York *Evening Post*, Nov. 20, Fol. 2.

A large crowd of "celebrities of literature and fashion attended." T's appearance corrected prevailing notions about his age and manners. Delivery was clear and without affectation. "Of the lecture as a work of art, it would be difficult to speak too strongly. . . . There has been nothing written about Swift so clever, and . . . we suspect one might add, nothing so unjust."

223.A [Bennett, James G.]. "Mr. Thackeray's First Public Appearance in America." New York *Herald*, Nov. 20, Fol. 1.
T is "the author of 'a book on snobs' and various other facetious productions of the same stamp." If Swift "could have heard the character given him by the 'snob biographer,' " he would have been "far from complimented."

224.A "Thackeray's Lectures." New York *Times*, Nov. 20, p. 4.
First lecture: "More attentive and delighted auditors never sat for an hour under an evening lecture. . . . T's fascination lies wholly in what he says—nothing of it is due to the way in which he says it." The treatment of Swift "was the most exquisite piece of biographical criticism and characterization."

225.A "Sketches of Lectures." New York Daily *Tribune*, Nov. 20, p. 5.
First lecture: The English journals have not done T justice in regard to elocution. "In short, his delivery was that of a well-bred gentleman." "The composition of his lecture was masterly. . . . It displayed the same subtle perception of character, and condensed vigor of expression, which distinguishes T above . . . all modern writers of fiction."

226.A "Thackeray's Lectures." New York *Times*, Nov. 23, p. 1.
The audience at the second lecture, in spite of bad weather, was larger than the first, and listened "with an even greater interest and a deeper satisfaction."

227.A "Sketches of Lectures." New York Daily *Tribune*, Nov. 23, p. 5.
T's elocution is even more agreeable when heard for the second time. "He elucidates the subject . . . in a manner which makes it clear to all classes of listeners."

228.A "Sketches of Lectures." New York Daily *Tribune*, Nov. 27, p. 5.
Third lecture: "Notwithstanding the violence of one of the worst rain storms of the year, . . . the house was full from desk to door."

229.A "Sketches of Lectures." New York Daily *Tribune*, Dec. 4, p. 5.
Fifth lecture: "For Hogarth and Smollett . . . he has little fellow feeling." But when he came to Fielding, T's English heart warmed to the subject, and he presented "one of the most splendid delineations of character."

230.A "Thackeray's Lectures." New York *Times*, Dec. 7, p. 1.
Following the report of the sixth lecture, all of the series are alluded to as "the finest productions of the day."

1853

Entries for this year are arranged chronologically, as usual, with the exception that the notices of T's lectures in the United States are grouped together before other entries. Reviews of the book EH (London or New York) appear in chronological order in the main section of the year's entries.

Notices of EH Lectures

(Only those are listed which make comments beyond reporting the text of the lecture.)

231.A "Mr. Thackeray's Lecture." Boston Daily *Courier*, Jan. 8, Fol. 2; Rptd. Semi-Weekly *Courier*, Jan. 10, Fol. 1.
Last lecture treated Sterne as "an unmitigated villain," and provided "a maudlin . . . stupid eulogy upon Goldsmith." T "was a humbug,—a mere retailer of old anecdotes and of fragments . . .—without originality, and . . . judgment."

232.A R[eed, Henry H.]. "Mr. Thackeray's Lectures." *North American & United States Gazette* (Phila.), Jan. 14, Fol. 1.
First lecture: E had already shown T's knowledge of the eighteenth century, but lecture proved how "charming it could be

made even without the aid of fiction." T's manner is pleasing by its simplicity.

233.A R[eed, Henry H.]. "Mr. Thackeray's Lectures." *North American & United States Gazette* (Phila.), Feb. 1, Fol. 1.
Upon completion of all lectures in Philadelphia: They were pleasing and instructive, and dealt with their subjects with a high moral tone, thus refuting the charges that they were not profound and introduced perilous writers.

234.A Richmond Daily *Whig*, March 4, Fol. 2.
First lecture: "Never have we read so caustic and withering a review of the life of . . . [Swift] as was given. . . . And the dexterious [*sic*] manner in which this was done, was something to remember. . . . T's style as a lecturer is the style of the finest passages in E, in P, and VF."

[235.]A Savannah Daily *Georgian*. From notices appearing March 14 through March 21, as reported by Harold S. Gulliver, "Thackeray in Georgia." *Georgia Review*, I (Sept. 1947), 35-43.
"Had not his books already done for him that service, his lectures would establish for T a most enviable reputation as a man of genius." Each of the lectures "seems to have been well nigh faultless in its way."

236.B "A Trio of Novels." *Dublin University Magazine*, XLI (Jan.), 70-79.
E surpasses previous novels as a work of art. Its domestic story is as important as the historical picture, which is basically sound despite inaccuracies. The characters, however, are really "creatures of the nineteenth century, dressed up in . . . quaint attire." T is more in his element when describing his own times.

237.B *Eclectic Review*, XCVII (Jan.), 37-49.
E will not enhance T's reputation. His tone remains the same and the characters have merely changed their costumes. A "clumsy and unintelligible" narrative, in which the antiquated style and the use of historical personages serves no good purpose. The marriage is a disappointing ending.

238.A *Graham's Magazine*, XLII (Jan.), 103.
E (New York) is somewhat inferior to P because "the story is more languid, the characters . . . less boldly represented." There is "no growth of interest, no development of plot," yet it is still fascinating, and Esmond is subtly portrayed. Rachel is T's finest woman.

239.A *Graham's Magazine*, XLII (Jan.), 105.
Brief notice of SGS (New York), remarking it as merely "an exhibition of rascality and ruffianism."

240.A [Mitchell, Donald G.]. "Editor's Easy Chair." *Harper's Magazine*, VI (Jan.), 271.
T's lectures have created a healthy interest in the eighteenth century, although "his satire seems more native than his eulogy is genial."

241.B "Mr. Thackeray and the Age of Queen Anne." *New Quarterly Review*, II (Jan.), 11-17.
E is a "marvellously incoherent work." T has wilfully misrepresented the men and manners of the time, and shows complete ignorance of basic history. He has produced only the haberdashery of the period. "The sooner we interdict . . . such trash the better."

242.A *Putnam's Monthly Magazine*, I (Jan.), 108.
E (New York) "has all the nice powers of observation and picturesqueness . . . but . . . it cannot have the freshness and truth of a novel relating to the present day."

243.A *Literary World*, XII (Jan. 8), 20-21; Rptd. *Living Age*, XXXVI (March 5), 434.
Reply to No. 220 above: Though there are parts of Fielding and Smollett, for example, which "we would not like to read aloud, to a sister, a daughter, or a son," overall there is "more virtue than vice." They are, moreover, significant authors and T could hardly ignore them. (See also Nos. 244, 245, and 249 below.)

244.A "Licentious Books Written By Men of Genius." New York *Recorder*, VIII (Jan. 19), 170; Rptd. *Living Age*, XXXVI (March 5), 435.
Continues debate started in No. 220 above: Admiration for

T cannot lessen the stricture that EH lectures called undue attention to a group of authors whose works are unfit for "young persons of both sexes." (See also No. 243 above and Nos. 245 and 249 below.)

245.A *Literary World*, XII (Jan. 29), 81-83; Rptd. *Living Age*, XXXVI (March 5), 435-436.
Reply to No. 244 above: Public expression about an author of Fielding's magnitude must be allowed especially when such appraisal, like T's, probes "every sore spot in . . . moral character." (See also Nos. 220, 243 above and No. 249 below.)

246.A *Graham's Magazine*, XLII (Feb.), 219-220.
FB and MG (New York), though minor works, are well calculated to amuse. FB is "delicious both for satire and sentiment."

247.A *National Era* (Washington, D. C.), VII, Feb. 3, p. 18.
BL (New York) "bears the image and superscription of T," and this is enough to commend it.

248.A *Literary World*, XII (Feb. 5), 102.
T's personal "courtesy and liberality" is praised for delivering the lecture "Humor and Charity," which "was a rather light, sketchy supplement to his [EH] lectures."

[249.]A "Reading Bad Books." New York *Recorder*, VIII (Feb. 23), 190.
(See Nos. 220, 243, 244, 245 above.)

250.B Alison, Archibald. "Thackeray and the Dickens School." *History of Europe*: From the Fall of Napoleon to the Accession of Louis Napoleon. 8 vols. Edinburgh: Blackwood, 1853-1859, I, Ch. 5, Sec. 70.
T is conspicuous by his great "graphic powers." But "satirical or humorous works, founded on the ridicule of passing manners, . . . rarely attain any lasting celebrity."

*251.B [Russell, Charles W.]. "The Novels of 1853." *Dublin Review*, XXXIV (March), 174-203.
Review of E. Prefatory remarks discuss state of the novel, and its need to veil some moral instruction. Of all satirists, T is the most earnest and scathing in his denunciation of vice,

but his writings are "dangerous to virtue in certain tempera-
ments." E is a good example of that "subtle tinge of fatalism"
in T's work which tends to "relax the . . . obligations of the
moral law." Esmond's weakness and blindness in his passion for Beatrix are unredeemable faults of character. Nor is
Rachel's marriage anything but improper.

252.A *Graham's Magazine*, XLII (March), 363.
BL (New York) is "powerfully and dramatically written."
T's use of irony and his insight are praised.

*253.A "Thackeray." *United States Magazine & Democratic Re-
view*, XXXII (March), 247-254.
E (New York), though an attempt at something great, is a
most complete failure, as almost all historical fiction must be,
because of its bookish rather than life-like quality. The story
itself is bad, especially the marriage because of the difference
in age. And Beatrix's end is "revolting and unnatural." T is
more "the great Scandal-Monger" than the great moralist,
and has gained a "cheap reputation" which sets a bad example to other writers. This influence is to be feared the
more "because he is essentially anti-republican. . . . There
cannot be found in all his work a single passage in which
tradesmen are mentioned with respect."

254.A *Literary World*, XII (March 12), 205-206.
Mr. Brown's Letters (New York) contains much milder observations than does S.

255.A "Mary L. Ware." *Putnam's Monthly Magazine*, I (April),
370-382.
Within this review of Mary Ware's biography, T is criticized
(pp. 371-373) for dividing women into two classes only—
the good-foolish and the selfish-shrewd. E is a moral improvement over both VF and P because of Esmond's noble
character. "In S, T exercises his genius legitimately and
curatively. . . . The whole civilized world should study it."
Moreover, T is praised for "the freedom of his books from
grossness and coarseness, in their technical sense."

256.A *Southern Literary Messenger*, XIX (April), 256.
Mr. Brown's Letters and NEH (New York) are "the very
best of T's minor compositions."

257.A *Southern Quarterly Review*, XXIII (April), 521-522.
E provides only glimpses of T's satiric vein and is not as satisfying as FB or YP. There is too much "unnecessary machinery" in the book. Its attraction lies in the historical portraits.

258.B [Martin, Theodore]. "Thackeray's Works." *Westminster Review*, N.S. III (April), 363-388; Rptd. *Living Age*, XXXVII (May 14), 387-399; *Eclectic Magazine*, XXIX (June), 141-155.
"Goodness, and candor, and generosity" have become less rare in T's work. Better experiences have tempered the "bitter and unfortunate" ones which can only explain the "pictures of tainted humanity" found, e.g., in YP. T's sentiment, when expressed, is genuine. "It is not cynicism . . . but a constitutional proneness to a melancholy view of life, which gives that unpleasing color to many of T's books." Latest work, E, is a literary feat but not fully alive.

259.A *National Era* (Washington, D. C.), VII, April 21, p. 62.
Brief notice of *Mr. Brown's Letters* (New York) commends T for his special preface, in which he politely notes the usual sharp practices of American publishers.

260.A *Graham's Magazine*, XLII (May), 635.
Mr. Brown's Letters (New York) "display great knowledge of society, and acutely satirize all . . . vanity, . . . and affectation."

261.A *Literary World*, XII (May 7), 378-380.
JD (New York) outdoes Smollett, Hood, and even Hook (*Ramsbottom Letters*) in the art of cacography.

262.A *Literary World*, XII (May 7), 380.
DB (New York), though depicting an English school, "is true to the experience of any similar scene in America."

263.A *National Era* (Washington, D. C.), VII, May 12, p. 75.
DB (New York) is "a playful but keen satire."

264.A *National Era* (Washington, D. C.), VII, May 26, p. 82.
JD (New York) and Reb are further examples of T's virtuosity at satire. Of all his works E alone is an exception to this strain and it "is very slow music, indeed."

265.A *Graham's Magazine*, XLII (June), 746.
Brief review of JD (New York), including Reb. JD is "the grossest caricature, but . . . caricature of genius." Reb is "a little dull" because too long.

266.B "Our Schools of Fiction. Thackeray As a Depicter of Character." *Hogg's Instructor*, N.S. X (June), 638-640.
The highest class of novelists "attempt simply to picture life." Thus T is greater than either Bulwer or Dickens. E is an example wherein T has "seen into the mechanisms of life," showing "the action of circumstance on the human mind." However, it is not a "pleasing novel." The love relationships are distasteful and "the religion is solely natural" rather than Christian.

267.A [Curtis, George W.]. "Thackeray in America." *Putnam's Monthly Magazine*, I (June), 638-642; Rptd. *Literary and Social Essays*. New York: Harper, 1895, pp. 127-145.
T made a better impression in America than Dickens did previously. The chief result of the visit was "that he convinced us of his intellectual integrity." The EH lectures were enjoyed principally because they were T's "impressions of those wits as men, rather than authors."

268.B [Forster, John]. *Examiner* (June 11), pp. 372-373; Rptd. *Living Age*, XXXVIII (July 30), 292-295.
EH, though not criticism in the strict sense, does contain masterly descriptive passages about the men's lives. The main fault is that the humorists are either "too much coaxed, patronized, or . . . abused."

269.B "Thackeray's English Humorists." *Spectator*, XXVI (June 11), 566; Rptd. *Living Age*, XXXVIII (July 30), 292.
Style and manner, as much as content, make EH worthwhile; though, perhaps, T has rated the eighteenth century too highly.

270.B [Chorley, Henry F.]. *Athenaeum* (June 18), pp. 732-733; (June 25), pp. 762-764.
Review of EH, noting that many facts could not be openly discussed because the lectures were originally delivered to a general audience. Swift is still a subject of controversy.

271.B *Morning Chronicle*, June 27, p. 3.
Review of EH. T's own gifts as a humorist qualify him as a
critic of his predecessors. No other book has done so much
to create an interest in the eighteenth century.

272.A [Ellis, George E.]. *Christian Examiner*, LV (July), 150.
EH is "filled with faithful sketches." "T understands those
men and their times better than any one else."

273.A *Harper's Magazine*, VII (July), 280.
EH (New York) reproduces the fascination of the lectures
themselves, which were without pretensions of being profound
criticism. Rather, they reveal personal aspects of T other
than those of satirist and cynic.

274.B "Thackeray's Lectures on the English Humorists." *New
Monthly Magazine*, XCVIII (July), 262-270; Rptd. *Eclectic
Magazine*, XXX (Dec.), 537-542.
EH is one-sided and presents distortions of Sterne and Ho-
garth, but is "full of sound, healthy, manly, vigorous writing
. . . in style pointed, clear, and straightforward."

*275.A [Kirk, John F.]. "Thackeray, As a Novelist." *North Amer-
ican Review*, LXXVII (July), 199-219.
T's only equals in penetrating motive and representing action
are Fielding and Jane Austen. His tone, even in early work,
indicates a "premature wisdom," a melancholy that is nevertheless strong and self-sustaining. T does not establish himself in the minds of characters, but remains among spectators,
"speculating on motive." But he is a "noisy spectator" and
this is an artistic defect, though also "the source of his originality and power." Women in his work, despite the impossibility of a man entering the female mind, display "virtues
and . . . foibles as are peculiarly feminine." One of his real
merits is "that he has not . . . put into one category the folly
that springs from love, and the folly that has its source in
selfish blindness." Though his irony "reminds us of Fielding's, . . . it is never, like Fielding's, sustained throughout
the work." But "in *range* of observation, T is certainly unrivalled."

276.A "Thackeray's English Humourists." *Southern Literary Messenger*, XIX (July), 437-444.
EH (New York) confirms the view created by the lectures that they "rank among T's best writing."

277.A *Southern Quarterly Review*, XXIV (July), 271.
DB (New York) shows T's ability as an artist and a chronicler of school-boy life.

278.B "Contemporary Literature of England." *Westminster Review*, N.S. IV (July), 269.
Review of EH: "Models of writing, if not of biography." Despite differences of opinion about the writers discussed, one can see in EH "a master's touch, the work of a true humourist."

279.A *Literary World*, XII (July 2), 523-525.
EH (New York) introduces "a new, gentlemanly, agreeable style of criticism," which will "break up the Carlyle pedantry," and which is "as effective, too, in the breaking up of a humbug."

280.B *Leader*, IV (July 9), 668.
EH "owes less to manner than we thought." Questionable as criticism, as essays "they are unaffectedly humourous, pathetic, subtle, . . . and thoughtful. . . . T's style . . . , half-sad, half-playful, is seen to perfection."

281.A *Graham's Magazine*, XLIII (Aug.), 221-222.
EH (New York) "lose something in being divorced from the lecturer's unusual voice and special manner." However, "the wit and sparkle of the style" come through. Americans can look T in the face because he has been paid for both the book and the lectures.

282.A "Thackeray's Women." *Knickerbocker*, XLII (Aug.), 155-159.
T's women are either composites of vice or flattering slaves, and they are thus unnatural. The fault springs from T's belief (stated in *Mr. Brown's Letters*) that what men want is "an exquisite slave . . . who . . . 'fondly lies to us through life.' " This notion is widespread and "has arisen from defective moral training in men for untold ages."

283.A *Knickerbocker*, XLII (Aug.), 185-187.
EH (New York) reflects the same qualities of observation and representation which mark T's novels of contemporary life. The past is truly re-created here.

284.A *National Era* (Washington, D. C.), VII, Aug. 4, p. 123.
EH (New York) is admirable because of T's sympathy with the era and the scrupulousness of his researches.

285.B *Athenaeum* (Oct. 1), p. 1158.
Brief notice of first no. of N. The opening fable and presentation of the family background is found to be confusing.

286.B Eagles, John. "Thackeray's Lectures—Swift." *Blackwood's Magazine*, LXXIV (Oct.), 494-518; Rptd. *Graham's Magazine*, XLIII (Dec.), 623-639; *Essays Contributed to Blackwood's Magazine*. Edinburgh: Blackwood, 1857.
EH does not contain biographical truth. The lecture on Swift, for example, shows T's distortion, as well as lack, of facts. At any rate, public lectures are no place for biography, since concessions to the audience are bound to be made.

287.A *Ladies Repository*, XIII (Oct.), 477.
EH (New York), like his novels, displays "the genial sunshine of T's wit." The natural grace and clarity of T's language make him a choice writer.

288.A "Charles Dickens: *Bleak House*." *North American Review*, LXXVII (Oct.), 409-439.
T discussed pp. 415-416: E, more than any previous work, will secure T's reputation with posterity. It does not, however, possess enough of that air of truthfulness of an eyewitness, but seems merely "hearsay evidence."

289.A *Putnam's Monthly Magazine*, II (Oct.), 452.
Though the tenor of T's new work (forthcoming N) and its array of characters can almost be forecast, it will be welcome. "'His works are like good sound old wine."

290.A *Southern Quarterly Review*, XXIV (Oct.), 541.
EH (New York) is amusing, but the knowledgeable reader will discover nothing new about the period.

291.B. *Spectator*, XXVI (Oct. 1), 949.
First no. of N "belies the prophesies . . . that 'the most respectable family' must be but a new form of the Baker Street 'snob.' " The fine style of VF and P is evident, as well as the artistic polish of E.

292.B *Leader*, IV (Oct. 8), 976.
First no. of N is "charming." "The satire is so delicate, so true, and yet so without bitterness."

293.B [Roscoe, William C.]. *Inquirer*, XII (Oct. 15), 659-660; (Oct. 22), 675-676; Second notice rptd. *Poems and Essays*. 2 vols. London: Chapman & Hall, 1860, II, 524-535.
Review of EH. "T is too strong for the work . . . , he has too powerful an impulse to create, and is . . . too full of himself and his own leanings to reflect any very accurate similitude of another." Nevertheless, the work is delightful and vivid.
Second notice deals wholly with Swift, whom T "judges hastily and imperfectly," thus doing great injustice.

294.A "Thackeray's New Novel." New York *Evening Post*, Oct. 22, Fol. 1.
Notice of first number of N endorses a London review that remarked N to be, "in all essential particulars, a continuation of P."

295.B "The English Humourists." *Prospective Review*, IX (Nov.), 468-487.
EH permits one to enter into familiar converse with great writers, guided by one of their own. T's "exquisitely natural and lucid style" commands respect even when there is disagreement in the appraisal. Reviewer agrees with T that literary men should not be treated differently from men in other professions.

296.A *Southern Literary Messenger*, XIX (Nov.), 701-706.
First no. of N begins well, though there is little development of the plot. T's return to the serial form is decried, especially since E proved so superior to other work "in point of finish."

297.A New York *Evening Post*, Nov. 5, Fol. 2.
T is taken to task for his aspersion of the American Revolution (Chap. 2, N). Even if his presence in the U.S. had not
taught him better, he should have suppressed comment for
the sake of prudence.

298.B *Times*, Nov. 22, p. 7.
Regret is expressed for T's injudicious reference to the American Revolution in N (Chap. 2). T is reminded "that already the majority of his readers are found on [the American]
side of the Atlantic." (See No. 297 above.)

1854

†299.A Bungay, George W. "Wm. Thackeray." *Off-Hand Takings*.
New York: DeWitt & Davenport, pp. 224-228.
Impressions of T when he lectured in Boston. EH is "not
darned and patched with epigrams, quips, quirks, or conun-
drums. . . . All figures rise up naturally out of the subject."

300.B [Senior, Nassau W.]. "Thackeray's Works." *Edinburgh Review*, XCIX (Jan.), 196-243; Rptd. *Living Age*, XL (March
11), 483-506; *Essays on Fiction*. London: Longman, Green,
1864, pp. 321-396.
VF is by far the best book—"sure of immortality"—though
it portrays only a limited side of life. Mean characters also
dominate P, in which, however, the field is wider. T asks
the reader to admire the unadmirable. This is a fault, as is
also his frequent personal intrusions. P lacks the historical
sense of time that VF has. E is "the imitation of an imitation." Its characters are detestable: Esmond, especially, for
making a revolution for a woman's sake. The marriage is
"neither natural nor pleasing." EH indicates that T is un-
familiar with the full canons of the authors considered.

301.B *New Quarterly Review*, III (Jan.), 5-6.
Family genealogies in first 2 nos. of N are tiresome, but in
No. 3 T "gets well into subject." In the portrayal of society,
"T has no rival in talent." Objections to T's reference to the
American Revolution (Chap. 2, N) have arisen because
Americans are "matter-of-fact people" who "do not under-
stand irony." (See Nos. 297 and 298 above.)

302.A [Curtis, George W.]. "Editor's Easy Chair." *Harper's Magazine*, VIII (May), 840-841.
N is "mellow and exquisite in tone." The harsher pre-VF style is subdued, though no wit or penetration is lost.

303.A [Curtis, George W.]. "Editor's Easy Chair." *Harper's Magazine*, IX (July), 259-260.
N is an accurate account of the world around us, and uses "none of the old hack machinery of novels." T's portrayal of Rev. Honeyman is defended on the grounds that T, like true clergymen, advocates rectitude and simplicity.

304.A Clarkson, Asher. "W. M. Thackeray." *Southern Literary Messenger*, XX (July), 385-395.
T is "the greatest novelist of the present age," because of his "fearless courage . . . to tell the disagreeable truth." His critics too often believe that man is better than he is in fact, and resent his depictions. His novels demand thought, and "the inferior class, forming the mass of readers," cannot appreciate his work.

305.B Gilfillan, George. "Thackeray." *A Third Gallery of Portraits*. Edinburgh: James Hogg, pp. 261-277.
EH shows T to be less great as a critic than he is as a novelist. He errs in calling Congreve and Pope, for example, humorists; also, in over-estimating the period.

306.B *Athenaeum* (Dec. 16), p. 1519.
RR "is a most sensible piece of nonsense"—a fairy tale that is "comically poetical."

307.B *Examiner* (Dec. 16), pp. 797-798.
RR praised without reservation as the "wittiest and most wonderful extravagance."

308.B *Leader*, V (Dec. 16), 1193-1194.
RR is praised for its fairy-tale quality, as well as its quiet satire of children's books in which morals are continually being drawn.

309.B *Spectator*, XXVII (Dec. 16), 1329-1330.
RR is "not witty, sentimental, humourous, or allegorical, but

simply funny." All its wisdom is contained in the hearty laugh it produces.

310.B *Morning Chronicle*, Dec. 28, p. 7.
RR is a "fairy-book . . . worthy to compare with . . . all the other immemorial favourites of the nursery . . . , but unlike them in insinuating . . . wise and useful lessons." Even here "T does not abandon his . . . task as censor of society."

1855

Entries for this year are arranged chronologically, as usual, with the exception that the notices of T's lectures in the United States are grouped together following other entries.

311.B [Oliphant, Margaret]. "Mr. Thackeray and His Novels." *Blackwood's Magazine*, LXXVII (Jan.), 86-96.
Bulwer is the "leader of the army of fiction" with T and Dickens "pressing close." T has progressed, both in his fiction and personally, in kindness and good humor, since earlier days. The tendency began in P and continues in N. In E, though, "our most sacred sentiments are outraged" when Rachel marries Esmond, in effect "her own devoted and respectful son." T's "greatest imperfection" is his inability to portray a woman as other than "an indiscriminate idolater of little children, and an angler for a rich husband."

312.B *Westminster Review*, N.S. VII (Jan.), 288.
RR can be compared to the works of Brentano, Tieck, Hauff, and Andersen, and T's ironic satire can still be found in every page.

313.A *Graham's Magazine*, XLVI (Feb.), 194.
Brief complimentary notice of RR.

314.B *Times*, March 23, p. 10.
"Charity and Humour" is the best lecture T ever delivered, because of its "firm grasp of a large subject, . . . poignancy, . . . humour, and . . . eloquent indignation."

315.B *Athenaeum* (Aug. 4), pp. 895-896.
N is "another attempt to define 'Respectability' as something different . . . from what the world dreams; another story of solemn dulness and smooth hypocrisy." More variety is expected from T. Also, he mars his work with his meandering comments. "A story, after all, should be a story, and not an essay."

316.B *Weekly Dispatch* (London), Aug. 12, p. 6.
Review of last no. of N. The colonel's death is a tragedy of pathos carried to majestic heights.

317.B *Spectator*, XXVIII (Aug. 18), 859-861.
N is a book in which goodness triumphs. Only those with "a faculty . . . for converting wholesome food into poison" will be able to misinterpret T's teaching.

318.B *Times*, Aug. 29, p. 5.
N surpasses previous novels in the variety of characters and in the fertility of invention. Stress is placed on the good characters, especially the colonel, "a noble creation, worthy of any age." T's chief defect is his lack of imagination—his restriction to pure facts. His gloomy view of life prevents his being a great novelist, and a lack of "spiritual sense" keeps him from the highest rank of artists, but his work will achieve "classical renown" nevertheless.

319.B *Examiner* (Sept. 1), pp. 548-549.
N is T's best work. Here, as in no former work, T explores "the depths of life and character," having a fuller opportunity to show "with how deep a sympathy he can approach all that is good; and speak of suffering and passion."

320.A [Godwin, Parke]. "Thackeray's *Newcomes*." *Putnam's Monthly Magazine*, VI (Sept.), 283-290; Rptd. *Out of the Past*. New York: Putnam, 1870, pp. 326-340.
N exemplifies T's principal qualities: a remarkable realism; a humor of great variety; and a seemingly effortless prose style that provides "a kind of unconscious flow of the author's thoughts." N also repudiates the charge of misanthropy levelled against T's work as well as the adverse criticism of his portraits of women. T's work truly seems to teach the love of truth and goodness for their own sakes.

*321.B [Elwin, Whitwell]. *Quarterly Review*, XCVII (Sept.), 350-378.

N is T's masterpiece. Here he portrays excellence as well as satirizing evil, continuing as ever to provide a "minute and faithful transcript of actual life." This depiction of "life under its ordinary aspects" does not imply lack of imagination, as many contend. It does, however, emphasize T's power as a moralist. "Unhallowed marriages . . . are the grand theme of the work." T's personal commentaries on the action are not defects, since they are such "signal beauties," and his language is so strong, easy and graceful.

322.B Friswell, Hain. "A Missing Chapter from *The Newcomes.*" *Sharpe's London Magazine*, N.S. VII (Sept.), 167-170.

T's apologetic and incomplete ending to N has disappointed readers; therefore, a chapter is written in which Laura arranges a sentimental reunion of Clive and Ethel, where each professes the long-hidden love for the other.

323.B "Mr. Thackeray and Charterhouse." *Examiner* (Sept. 8), p. 566.

T's portrayal of Charterhouse (as Grey Friars) in N is false, in that it represents the place as far more pleasant, comfortable, and well-managed than it was at the time depicted.

324.B [Hannay, James]. *Leader*, VI (Sept. 8), 870-871.

Review of N prefaced by remarks on the truth of T's fiction, its significance as a reflection of the age, and as a moral beacon. N is not as good a story as VF, but depicts "a quieter and more decent kind of life." Goodness is made beautiful, though not necessarily fortunate, which, moreover, is the usual case in the present social system.

325.B *New Quarterly Review*, IV (Oct.), 423-428.

N is T's greatest work. It shows that he has "genial sympathy for his fellow creatures" and that the edge of his satire "cuts only against wrong and ignorance." Because he is not didactic, he has been misunderstood; people in general prefer "a rose-water sentimentalism" to the truth.

*326.A "Thackeray." New York *Times*, Oct. 29, p. 2; Rptd. *Home Journal*, Nov. 10, Fol. 1; *Living Age*, XLVII (Dec. 1), 562-565.

T is welcomed on the eve of his lectures. There is unqualified admiration for the man, in spite of critical reservations about his work. T-Dickens comparison is unnatural and unfair, because Dickens is a reformer and "T's genius is simply negative." "Severe and courageous truth" is his main virtue, and his "great fault is his total absence of poesy."

327.B [Patmore, Coventry]. "Fielding and Thackeray." *North British Review*, XXIV (Nov.), 197-216; Rptd. *Living Age*, XLVII (Dec. 29), 769-779; *Eclectic Magazine*, XXXVII (Jan. 1856), 57-69.
Review of N. T, like Fielding, can present human nature so fully that even discreditable characters claim kindred with us; however, it is not true that T inclines towards mean characters. Certainly not in N, where goodness prevails. "T is almost the only modern writer who has understood that the secret of describing . . . a true woman is to do it by negatives." T is correct in being more reticent than Fielding in depicting certain behavior.

328.B [Rands, William B.]. "Apropos of Mr. Thackeray." *Tait's Edinburgh Magazine*, N.S. XXII (Nov.), 670-677.
"T is . . . the most painful of authors." He performs great service by denouncing pretense, but is not "speaking the truth in love, as a prophet should." As a "Realist . . . , he must take his place below an Idealist of even less talent" (e.g. Dinah Mulock). T's principal defect: "He seems to have no perception of CONSCIENCE as a supreme, regulating principle in human character."

329.B *Athenaeum* (Nov. 10), pp. 1301-1302; Rptd. *Living Age*, XLVIII (Jan. 12, 1856), 114-115.
Miscellanies, Vol. I, is a valuable addition to T's publications.

330.B *Leader*, VI (Nov. 10), 1083-1084.
Miscellanies, Vol. I, "show the early forms of a talent now everywhere admired; . . . of a mind now justly regarded as one of the most remarkable in English literature." S is one of T's best works.

331.B "The Writings of W. M. Thackeray." *Hogg's Instructor*, 3rd ser. V (Dec.), 425-437.
Truth in observation and satirical wit were responsible for

T's initial popularity. He has shown progress in skill as a novelist as well as developing "more enlarged views of human nature." The brighter picture of life began in P and finds fulfillment in N, through such characterizations as the colonel and Laura.

332.A "Thackeray as a Poet." *Putnam's Monthly Magazine,* VI (Dec.), 623-627.
T's ballads "have the same deep, human sympathy, that warms his books. . . . They are full of . . . hearty and genuine democracy."

333.B [Maine, Henry S.]. "Mr. Thackeray and the Four Georges." *Saturday Review,* I (Dec. 15), 106-107.
T errs in his duty as a British citizen by delivering FG lectures in America where they will undoubtedly be misinterpreted.

Notices of FG Lectures

(Only those are listed which make comments beyond reporting the text of the lecture.)

334.A [Bennett, James G.]. "Mr. Thackeray on George the First." New York *Herald,* Nov. 2, p. 4.
"We do not report T's lectures simply because they are not worth reporting. . . . There is no more research or labor required to get up a lecture like that of T on George I than to prepare many of the articles which appear in the *Herald.*"

335.A "Mr. Thackeray's Lectures." New York *Times,* Nov. 2, p. 1.
Though "excellent . . . , noble in sentiment, and brilliant in episode," the lecture on George I was not as interesting as some of the EH lectures.

336.A "Mr. Thackeray's Lectures." New York *Tribune,* Nov. 2, p. 5.
George I did not excite the same interest as EH, though it is apparent that T took "great care in preparing the lecture." Also commendable was T's "honest, heartfelt tone of indignation" against "these wretched little tyrants."

337.A "Mr. Thackeray's Lectures." New York *Times*, Nov. 6, p. 4. George II: The "fierce onslaught" of criticism against T is unjustified, even though EH lectures were better. The main defect is T's lack of historical perspective, in place of which he substitutes gossip.

338.A "Mr. Thackeray's Lectures." New York *Tribune*, Nov. 6, p. 5.
Second lecture was more interesting than first. Though T deals more with small gossip than with fact, the basic truth-fulness is evident. "We are delighted then to see good and sincere men like T wrestle with historical characters."

339.A "Mr. Thackeray's Lectures." New York *Times*, Nov. 9, p. 8. T seemed to hurry over the reign of George III, without touching on much important matter.

340.A [Willis, Nathaniel P.]. "Thackeray's Lectures." *Home Journal*, Nov. 10, Fol. 2.
Though the subject might have been a dull one for an American audience, T created an "atmosphere of vivid romance. And yet he never appears to transcend the limits of historic truth."

341.A "Mr. Thackeray's Lectures." New York *Tribune*, Nov. 10, p. 7.
The epoch of George III seemed more distinctly created than those previous. T's portrait of the King stands comparison to that of Macaulay's William.

342.A "Mr. Thackeray's Lectures." New York *Tribune*, Nov. 13, p. 5.
George IV lecture was less interesting because there was less of T in it, and also less of a picture of the times.

343.A "Mr. Thackeray's Lectures." New York *Times*, Nov. 14, p. 2. Lecture on George IV was long and rambling and "entirely deficient in wholeness." The reference to George Washington was unnecessary "clap-trap," since we all know how great a man Washington was.

344.A *Putnam's Monthly Magazine*, VI (Dec.), 663-664.
FG lectures needed more unity and nobler characters. They were as "formless, discursive, rambling as the plots of his novels."

1856

Entries for this year are arranged chronologically, as usual, with the exception that the notices of T's lectures in the United States are grouped together before other entries. Notices of T's lectures in Great Britain are listed at the end of the year but do not disturb the chronological sequence of other entries.

Notices of FG Lectures

(Only those are listed which make comments beyond reporting the text of the lecture.)

345.A "Mr. Thackeray's Lectures." Philadelphia *Bulletin*, Jan. 3, Fol. 2.
First lecture: "The tone of the sarcasm was too uninterrupted."

346.A "Mr. Thackeray." Philadelphia *Bulletin*, Jan. 5, Fol. 4.
Second lecture was no more than "polished scurrility," with much sarcasm and little good humor. T presented the "corruptions of that time . . . stirred up in all their festering putridity. . . ."

347.A *North American & United States Gazette* (Phila.), Jan. 5, Fol. 2.
First lecture provided "keen comment on the shams of royalty and the realities of vice."

348.A "Mr. Thackeray." Philadelphia *Bulletin*, Jan. 7, Fol. 2.
Though the sarcasm was less obtrusive, the third lecture "was singularly barren of new ideas." In general, the lectures are merely "a recapitulation of the petty gossip and indecent scandals of the times."

349.A "Mr. Thackeray's Georges." *North American & United States Gazette* (Phila.), Jan. 7, Fol. 2.
On the evening of the last lecture, T's truth about the Georges is praised. The charge that he would be afraid to deliver such talks in England is condemned as absurd.

350.A "Mr. Thackeray's Last Lecture." Philadelphia *Bulletin*, Jan. 8, Fol. 4.
In content and method, T "outraged decency, common sense and logic." He affronted the parent-hearers by explaining George IV's libertinism in terms of a too-strict upbringing. "It was for a nation of 'snobs' he was writing, when he prepared these lectures for America. . . . He left his reputation safely at home."

351.A *Southern Literary Messenger*, XXII (Feb.), 156.
Lectures in Richmond, Va., provided pleasure and instruction, though "inferior in interest . . . to EH because devoted to subjects less congenial." Nevertheless, court life was depicted with detail "made pungent with . . . mordant wit."

[352.]A Savannah *Daily Morning News,* Feb. 15; as reported in T's *Letters and Private Papers,* ed. G. N. Ray (Cambridge, Mass., 1945-1946), III, 553.
Second lecture drew the largest audience "ever assembled in a lecture room in Savannah." As "litterateur and lecturer," T is highly appreciated.

[353.]A *Georgia Journal & Messenger* (Macon, Ga.), Feb. 27; as reported in T's *Letters and Private Papers,* ed. G. N. Ray (Cambridge, Mass., 1945-1946), III, 571.
The lectures as well as T himself made "a very favorable impression." "The last one in particular seemed to delight everybody present."

354.A New Orleans *Picayune*, March 8, Fol. 2.
First lecture was "a graphically sketched panorama" of the period, and full of "dazzling analysis."

355.A New Orleans *Picayune*, March 11, Fol. 2.
Second lecture shows T at his best "in turning inside out a hollow sham. . . . Such exuberant expletiveness of satire, such

pleonastic affluence of denunciation, never before were known to mark the strictures of a critic."

356.A New Orleans *Picayune*, March 13, Fol. 2.
Third lecture was pitched in a lower key because the reign of George III was so dull itself.

---

*357.A T[uckerman], H[enry] T. "Mr. Thackeray As a Novelist."
Christian Examiner, LX (Jan.), 102-121.
"T seizes on the broad follies and selfish instincts of human nature," and though his depiction may be true, "it is not healthful." He fails to represent "the earnest side of life, and the disinterested and humane sympathies." His characters are either "monsters" or "flats." This lack of "profound" insight is obvious especially in the portrayal of women. E is literary art, but the love theme "is a perversion which sickens the heart." Even N, for all its detail of fact, is an unreliable picture of life: "The good people in it are so weak, the bad so absurd."

358.A [Curtis, George W.]. "Editor's Easy Chair." *Harper's Magazine*, XII (Jan.), 262-264.
FG lectures were disappointing. They were "collections of court gossip" more than analyses of the times through appreciation of the men, as EH were. However, the charge that T tried to appear as a democrat is absurd.

359.B [Roscoe, William C.]. "W. M. Thackeray, Artist and Moralist." *National Review*, II (Jan.), 177-213; Rptd. *Poems and Essays*. 2 vols. London: Chapman & Hall, 1860, II, 264-308.
T is a great "painter of manners, not of individual men," failing to penetrate "the interior, secret, *real* life that every man leads in isolation from his fellows. . . . T only desires to be a mirror. . . . His conception of a story is . . . incomplete." There is an absence of "ideas" in his work. "As a moralist, his philosophy might be called a religious stoicism rooted in fatalism." He is a "sceptic of principles of human will." N, "the most humane work," still has the "see-saw between cynicism and sentiment, the same suspension of moral judgement."

360.B *New Quarterly Review*, V (Jan.), 25-28; (Oct.), 411-413.
Review of *Miscellanies*, Vols. I-III. Time has mellowed T's
harsher early attitudes. S is "the gem of . . . T's fugitive
works." It influenced real improvements in behavior and
helped lessen humbug and affectation. (25-26) In BL, "the
moral is sound, and the art is marvelous." (413)

361.A [Peabody, A. P.]. *North American Review*, LXXXII (Jan.),
284.
N is by far T's best work. The "humane" takes precedence
over the scornful. The leading characters command sympathy and, in the case of the colonel, reverence.

362.B [Burne-Jones, Edward]. "Essay on *The Newcomes*." *Oxford and Cambridge Magazine*, I (Jan.), 50-61; Rptd. *Bibelot*, IV (Oct. 1898), 321-359.
The charge that T largely portrays evil is foolish; especially
since novels are not merely for entertainment, but provide
"our real education." N focuses on the problems of bad marriages and the pressure of fashion or convention. "T has done
good service to truth of morality and fact."

363.B *Leader*, VII (Jan. 5), 19.
Review of *Miscellanies*, Vol. II. Better selection of the early
periodical pieces should have been exercised. NEH, the
best of the pieces, is a supreme example of parody.

364.A *Graham's Magazine*, XLVIII (Feb.), 171.
Ballads (Boston) do T no discredit. The poems are artistic
and the rhymes good, "but . . . T has not the soul of a poet."

365.B "Mr. Thackeray's Ballads." *Chambers's Journal*, XXV (Feb.
2), 73-76; Rptd. *Living Age*, XLIX (April 19), 142-145.
Review of *Miscellanies*, Vol. IV. T's poems prove "how good,
how great a man we have amongst us." They are satirical
and yet "full of pathos, full of hearty humanity." Somewhat
on the model of Hood.

366.A 'Lorris' [pseud. of William G. Simms]. Charleston *Mercury*,
Feb. 27, Fol. 2.
N is full of "vitality . . . , quiet satire . . . , and goodly human
traits." T's ability to present minute social details is also what
popularizes his FG lectures, which otherwise are "little more
than well-arranged gossip."

367.A *Graham's Magazine*, XLVIII (April), 370.
Ballads (Boston) exhibit all the qualities of T—satire, caricature, wit, etc.—which, however, are found to better advantage in his novels.

*368.A *Christian Examiner*, LX (May), 439-445.
T's right to the name novelist is questioned, because none of his works, from YP to N, fulfills the strict conditions of a novel: a carefully arranged opening and the development of a complicated and interlacing plot. Likewise his work "may prove unwholesome," misleading the young to accept "his caricatures for realities, and his cynicism for penetration." Good characters in N do not redeem it, since it is when T writes in his own person that he indulges in the skeptical spirit. N is "diffuse and wearisome, abounding with scraps of all sorts of plundered prose and verse . . . and of no language that is in use among gentlemen." T's books suffer in comparison with those of Dickens.

*369.B [Oakeley, Frederick]. *Dublin Review*, XL (June), 299-309.
N presents a more "amiable picture of social life," but not a truer one than VF. T's works are "more serviceable to the cause of morality, . . . because they . . . [do not imply] that *mere* natural virtue is *adequate* even to the ordinary casualties." T's disdain of the world and his hatred of cant "betoken . . . a condition of mind, to the qualities of which the Catholic religion is singularly fitted."

370.B [Cracroft, Bernard]. "Thackeray and Currer Bell." *Oxford and Cambridge Magazine*, I (June), 323-335.
"A fragrance of philanthropy lies beneath the often bitter leaves of T's writings." He is misunderstood because a satirist must describe the exception and not the rule. *Jane Eyre* and T's work both share in public condemnation, yet both are forces for good. The former shows moral heroism in an ordinary nature, and T divests heroism of supposedly heroic characters.

371.A *National Era* (Washington, D. C.), X, Aug. 21, p. 133.
Ballads (Boston) are "pleasant to read" without making claim to any high order of poetic merit.

372.B "Mr. Thackeray." *Scotsman* (Edinburgh), Nov. 1, Fol. 2.
Welcome to T on eve of FG lectures. His fame has been "fairly and gallantly won." E is "the most finished bit of 'feigned history' in our language."

373.B "Mr. Thackeray's Lecture." *Scotsman* (Edinburgh), Nov. 5, Fol. 3.
First lecture: "T presented . . . vivid pictures of bygone life and manners which, almost as much as the depth of his insight into human character and motives, give him pre-eminence as a lecturer."

374.B "Mr. Thackeray on the Four Georges." *Chambers's Journal*, XXVI (Dec. 6), 353-355; Rptd. *Living Age*, LII (Jan. 24, 1857), 205-208.
Report of the favorable reception of the lectures in Scotland and the U.S. However, FG is indicative of T's tendency to select bad types of humanity for the amusement of the public.

375.B [Stephen, James F.]. *Saturday Review*, II (Dec. 27), 783-785.
Review of BL. "In some respects . . . the most characteristic and best executed of T's works." It has the advantage of brevity, and thus "the plot is clearer, simpler, and more connected than . . . in VF, P, or N. . . . The book has a moral . . . but it is kept in its proper place."

Notices of FG Lectures in London

376.B "Mr. Thackeray's Lectures." *Daily News*, Dec. 31, p. 2.
First lecture, "lively, spirited, and entertaining as it is, leaves behind it an impression of sadness. Nothing can be more dark and gloomy than its view of human life."

377.B "Mr. Thackeray's Lectures on the Four Georges." *Morning Chronicle*, Dec. 31, p. 3.
First lecture: "In these brilliant sketches of the life and manners of our forefathers, T has the same keen eye for the follies and foibles of the time that his novels display with respect to his own day."

378.B "Mr. Thackeray's Lectures." *Times*, Dec. 31, p. 6.
First lecture: T's charm and sarcastic humor provided "a solemnity of irreverence in his discourse that may be compared to the tone of Gibbon."

1857

Notices of FG Lectures in London (cont.)

379.B "Thackeray on the Georges." *Leader*, VIII (Jan. 3), 15.
First lecture: T's account of the age is in the manner of Hogarth, but with more tenderness and refinement. He draws parallels between contemporary vices and those of the earlier age, but "the influence of his satire is limited, because he speaks above the heads of the vulgar."

380.B [Sandars, Thomas C.]. "Mr. Thackeray on George the First." *Saturday Review*, III (Jan. 3), 11.
Lecture was not unworthy of T. However, it is acceptable only as light entertainment, not as serious history. It "bears traces of having been originally intended for the American market. The jeers at lords and kings . . . must have sounded sweetly on republican ears."

381.B "Mr. Thackeray." *Spectator*, XXX (Jan. 3), 9.
First lecture: "A mine of solid thought couched beneath a surface of irony." T's humor is too subtle to be "appreciated . . . by a multitude unused to the most delicate forms of sarcasm."

382.B "Mr. Thackeray's Lectures." *Daily News*, Jan. 7, p. 5.
Second lecture: T "ransacked" historical documents about George II "and what a 'Vanity Fair' has he made of the whole!"

383.B "Mr. Thackeray's Lectures." *Times*, Jan. 14, p. 10.
Third lecture was "free from that severity by which the first two were characterized." T's eloquent prose-lyric on George's madness "gave to the hitherto comical figure the tragic dignity of a Lear or an Oedipus."

384.B "Mr. Thackeray's Lectures." *Morning Post,* Jan. 21, p. 6.
Full series: In his exposé of the lives and times of the Georges,
T proceeded, with his usual abusive approach, to "pillory
everyone who rose prominently above the surface of society."

385.B "Mr. Thackeray's Lectures." *Times,* Jan. 21, p. 8.
Fourth lecture: "The merit of being the first to make an un-
illustrated lecture the cause of 'crush' is entirely due to T."

386.A *Southern Literary Messenger,* XXIV (Feb.), 151-158.
Miscellanies mainly show "a predominance of the critical faculty" and "a cool and discriminative judgment" rather than
"a creative mind." But no other author is "more true to the
appropriate manners and characters" of the century. BL,
however, shows creativity. "This is almost pure art without
the help of photography." The ballads "would have made
the reputation of any other poet by profession."

387.A Bayne, Peter. "The Modern Novel: Dickens—Bulwer—
Thackeray." *Essays in Biography and Criticism.* First Series.
Boston: Gould & Lincoln, pp. 363-392.
T breaks with the conventions of novel writing so daringly
"that he goes too far, and puts in peril the essence of his Art.
. . . The non-existent Pickwick will always be more deeply
loved than the actual Dobbin. . . . T owes his popularity to
reviewers. The men who were not in the way of experiencing
emotion recognized his powers." His realism will exert a
good influence in fiction, but "it is a pre-Raphaelite school of
novel writing," and, as such, cannot be an end in itself.

388.B [Hannay, James]. *Athenaeum* (Oct. 3), pp. 1229-1231.
Miscellanies present early works which reveal the growth of
T's mind. His style proves him "one of the healthiest writers
. . . since the days of Scott and Byron." Theme and observation take precedence over story. S is an example of the
justice in T's writings and GHD illustrates a "certain vein of
tenderness."

389.B. *Examiner* (Nov. 7), pp. 709-710.
Brief notice of first no. of V. "The beginning . . . promises
well. . . . Its temper wise and kindly." Countess Bernstein
praised as a portrait of Beatrix grown old.

390.B *Leader*, VIII (Nov. 7), 1072.
First no. of V is greeted warmly. T's use of characters who relate to others already developed in other books is praised for its naturalness and the sense of reality it conveys.

391.B *Spectator*, XXX (Nov. 7), 1178.
First no. of V shows T's "clearness of style . . . together with an easy unobtruded knowledge of the age." The satire here, as usual, is likely to offend, because some of it seems gratuitous.

392.B *Leader*, VIII (Dec. 12), 1191.
New edition of E should be read as introduction to V. T's best work is "of man as seen in society. . . . Dickens is the poet . . . of humanity. . . . T is the poet of society."

†393.B Crispe, Thomas E. *Thackeray, Humorist and Satirist.* London: Wm. Davy.
Originally a lecture, largely on VF, especially the character of Becky. "T has two great faults,—his bad opinion of the world, and his want of appreciation of women." Nevertheless he is a fearless critic of past and present faults.

1858

394.A [Thompson, John R.]. "Editor's Table." *Southern Literary Messenger*, XXVI (Jan.), 75-77.
First eight chapters of V give "the promise of a most interesting story," but as yet are not very animated or entertaining. Undoubtedly T's "dreadful satire" will illumine human weaknesses. It is hoped, however, that he will be able to deal also "with some of the loftiest manifestations of the nobility of nature," e.g. George Washington. At least one anachronism has already occurred, and the historic fidelity in general is below the standard of E.

395.A [Thompson, John R.]. "Editor's Table." *Southern Literary Messenger*, XXVI (Feb.), 152-153.
T's "carelessness and improper freedom" in Chaps. 9-12 of V add more historical inaccuracies. (See No. 394 above.) The worst fault involves the attempt to introduce Washington as more than a passing reference.

396.A [Curtis, George W.]. "The Lounger." *Harper's Weekly*, II (Feb. 20), 114-115.
T is both respectful and basically accurate in his portrayal of Washington (in V), who "was not a demi-god" nor merely "a prudent and accurate machine."

397.A [Curtis, George W.]. "Editor's Easy Chair." *Harper's Magazine*, XVI (March), 558-559.
The argument of No. 396 above is repeated.

398.B Vaughan, Robert A. "Thackeray's *Esmond*." *Essays and Remains*. 2 vols. London: Parker, II, 311-320.
"E is the worst in plot and best in expression of all T's writings. Female character is even less charitably treated than in former fictions." Though genealogy is confusing, the book succeeds in its disguise as family memoir. Esmond is "capable of self-sacrifice, yet destitute of . . . ardor and . . . strength. . . . With an almost female facility, he is led . . . by his feelings." Such a man is a questionable hero. The unpleasant dénouement "in hands less capable would have been simply repulsive."

*399.B Jeaffreson, John C. "William Makepeace Thackeray." *Novels and Novelists*: From Elizabeth to Victoria. 2 vols. London: Hurst & Blackett, II, 262-281.
The development of the novel in the nineteenth century is traced, showing how T satisfied the craving for "something more *truthful* in fiction." Dickens "is as deceitful . . . and wittingly dishonest a describer as can be found. . . . The triumph of his art is in the perfection of his deceit." T, however, made "simplicity and accuracy without reserve" his chief characteristics. The charge of cynicism is merely society's reaction to being confronted with the unpleasant truth. "T's success is almost solely owing to his moral influence," in contrast to Dickens', which is based on his art. Compared with Fielding, T has "a less genial temper, . . . a less subtle humour," but he has a "kind of religious fervour" which Fielding lacked.

400.B "Gentlemen Authors." *Saturday Review*, VI (July 17), 55-56; Rptd. *Living Age*, LVIII (Sept. 4), 742-744.
Regarding the Yates affair and charges of ungentlemanly conduct: If it was a descent on Yates's part to write the sketch

of T, it was especially a descent for T to give public lectures
where all who would pay could "peep at him."

401.A [Curtis, George W.]. "The Lounger." *Harper's Weekly,* II
(July 31), 483.
First third of V reveals T's skill in presenting character as
well as the perfection of the historical sense and setting. Plot
is always at a minimum in his work, and thus its absence is
not to be criticized.

402.B [Dixon, Hepworth]. *Athenaeum* (Oct. 23), pp. 515-516.
Review of V, Vol. I. T preaches a good deal, but "most of
these sermons are delightful for their insight and their satire."

1859

403.B Masson, David. "British Novelists Since Scott." *British Novelists and Their Styles.* Cambridge: Macmillan, pp. 229-253,
257-259.
Discussion and comparison of T's and Dickens' styles, essentially incorporating the views in No. 148 above. T is con-
servative, attacking personal rather than social abuses. The
growth of "a wholesome spirit of Realism" in novel writing
comes largely from the influence of T.

404.B [Smith, Goldwin]. *Edinburgh Review,* CX (Oct.), 438-453.
"V is neither antiquarian nor, in the strict sense, historical."
T misapplies his powers in this hybrid sort of composition.
The age portrayed in V was already presented by its contemporary writers with far greater freedom of expression. The
use of historical persons in the novel is questionable. T's
"wild oats" theory, again presented, flouts common sense.
A man does not learn control by giving way to low passions
in his youth.

405.B [Kent, Charles]. "W. M. Thackeray—Satirist and Humorist."
Dublin University Magazine, LIV (Nov.), 630-640; LV (Jan.
1860), 22-35; Rptd. *Footprints on the Road.* London:
Chapman & Hall, 1864, pp. 370-407.
Biographical outline proceeds from book to book up to VF.
Early work showed T's capacity as an art critic and fiction
reviewer. GHD was first strong book. ISB prejudiced and

out of date now. CC shows an offensive combination of cynicism and skepticism. "The peculiar combination in T's genius . . . [is] the distinctive and vividly contrasting attitudes of the Satirist and the Humorist"—"as if his pen . . . dropped honey and vitriol." VF is the crowning example of this quality.

406.A [Curtis, George W.]. "Editor's Easy Chair." *Harper's Magazine*, XIX (Nov.), 840-841.
Praise for V (upon its completion) because it "shows the same heart and eye and hand that all the rest of his works show."

407.B *Saturday Review*, VIII (Nov. 19), 610-612.
Review of V, but discussing T generally. The substance of each successive novel is precisely the same. They adopt a view of life which is accurate though shallow. T writes as a gentleman and has neither debased nor insulted his generation, but his avoidance of portraying greatness as well as "the common business of life" prevented him from writing the great epic of his own age.

408.A *Southern Literary Messenger*, XXIX (Dec.), 475.
V (New York) evades classification as either an historical or a society novel. In fact, it is "hardly . . . a novel at all, for story there is none." What is worse is the "undue freedom taken with fact, in historical and geographical matters." The book's only charm is T's wonderful style.

409.B *Examiner* (Dec. 3), p. 772.
Review of V. Though there is the usual deficiency of plot, this is T's method and he must be permitted to pursue it. His strength here, as in previous work, is "reality of presentment." Also in V "a wise tone of kindliness blends more and more with his sarcasm."

410.B [Dallas, Eneas S.]. *Times*, Dec. 16, p. 7.
Review of V. Historical fiction helps T escape from charge of severity and also lets him make the point that men are not dissimilar in motive. V's fault, if any, is that T tries to include too much: Balance between the two brothers' stories is lost. T has outlived the false charge of cynicism and will outlive the

prudery in much criticism. He ranks beside Scott; and, as a moralist, above all fiction writers.

*411.B *Daily News*, Dec. 30, p. 2.
Review of V, and a defense of historical fiction. T's lectures and research qualify him to present the historical period with "telling minuteness of detail." And yet V is clearly an expression of the nineteenth century. It is both good and necessary that T writes in a less coarse vein than the eighteenth-century authors. The use of historical personages in V is good (See No. 404 above) and all other characters are completely and strikingly developed.

1860

412.A [Ware, L. G.]. "Novels of 1859." *Christian Examiner*, LXVIII (Jan.), 113-124.
V (New York), though not the equal of VF and E in careful artistic construction, does bear out the prestige of T. That he repeats himself is not a fault as long as charm, style, and humor are there. The picture of Colonial life is marked with "faithfulness of detail" as well as a "truthfulness of its display of the minds and hearts of women in those days."

[413.]A [Simms, William G.]. Charleston *Mercury*, Jan. 5; as reported in *Letters of William Gilmore Simms*. ed. Mary Oliphant and others. 5 vols. Columbia, S. C.: Univ. of South Carolina, 1952-1956, IV, 187n.
V (New York) shows T's powers of "construction," "quiet satire," and "insight into human frailties," but "the bad and base . . . are allotted, as usual, too large a proportion of its pages." The worst fault is the portrait of Washington. Not only did T lack historical knowledge, but he shows that his feelings were neither with the American people nor with Washington, who was "not the mere hero of the country—but its sainted model man."

414.A *Ladies Repository*, XX (Feb.), 122.
Notice of V (New York). "We have not read it entire. We are acquainted with no one who has read it. . . . We have no doubt it combines some of the best qualities as well as the greatest defects of its author."

415.B "Orders of Merit." *Saturday Review,* IX (May 12), 596-598.
RP essay about an English Legion of Honor (*Cornhill,* I, 631-640) is criticized because of T's high-handed manner of disposing of the issue. His wide influence is regretted, since it helps broadcast such vapid and inconsistent feelings.

416.A *Southern Literary Messenger,* XXXI (Aug.), 159.
L (New York) is very close to what might be called " 'slop-shop' work." Its merit of being short would be improved if it had not been written at all. "T is becoming tiresome. There is an intolerable sameness about him."

417.A S[hearer], S[extus]. "Major Arthur Pendennis." *Yale Literary Magazine,* XXV (Aug.), 383-387.
A literary dissection of the Major reveals him to be the epitome of "irreproachable hypocrisy."

418.A [Curtis, George W.]. "The Lounger." *Harper's Weekly,* IV (Aug. 4), 483.
FG (New York) are negative examples of conduct, and also "are invaluable in destroying any foolish prestige that may chance to surround royalty."

419.A [Luyster, I. M.]. "The Women of Thackeray." *Christian Examiner,* LXIX (Sept.), 167-190.
An understanding of T's style is necessary in order to "detect the great humanity under the surface cynicism." An examination of the women in VF, P, E, N, and V shows that they are not "misty shapes," but "life-like creations" that are truly feminine. Lady Castlewood, for example, is a woman whom "age cannot wither." Her virtues as well as her faults are womanly, and there is no incongruity in her union with Esmond.

420.A Felton, Cornelius C. *North American Review,* XCI (Oct.), 580-582.
T's introduction of Washington in V was "rash and infelicitous," and results in complete failure. "The sarcastic delineator of vice and follies" (he who "has never drawn a true and dignified woman, nor a gentleman of the highest type") could never comprehend a simple, pure, and noble man. Portrait is riddled with anachronisms. The worst "moral blunder" was to have shown Washington drawn into a duel.

421.B [Palgrave, Francis T.]. "W. M. Thackeray as Novelist and Photographer." *Westminster Review*, N.S. XVIII (Oct.), 500-523.
T's cynicism, as well as his limited view, his failure in art, and the "absence of forcible thought" are ascribed to his method, which is the equivalent of photography in producing literal detail without distinction. E and N, however, make "a claim to high art." In V, too, "T shows himself a creative artist . . .; preserving his minute accuracy, and yet rising above it to larger truth."

422.A [Curtis, George W.]. "Editor's Easy Chair." *Harper's Magazine*, XXII (Dec.), 122.
FG (New York) draw more upon the social gossip than upon the literature or history of the epoch.

*423.A C. "Thackeray Versus Dickens." *Southern Literary Messenger*, XXXI (Dec.), 445-449.
Both authors are beginning to falter. V and L indicate this about T. Still, T is a better moralist and the view that he "takes a narrow view of mankind" is absurd, as is shown by P and N. The idea started with VF, but that is not a novel—only a satire. "T's is essentially a Christian philosophy," because it accepts the world without "attempting to gauge the justice of infinite Deity." Dickens' good characters are merely "flatteries of the human race," and his evil monsters deny the possibility of anyone becoming like them. "Dickens makes man perfect in his own strength." He is a heathen philosopher. T reminds us that a person's trials do not end with marriage, or at any other time in life.

1861

424.A [Curtis, George W.]. "Editor's Easy Chair." *Harper's Magazine*, XXII (Feb.), 414-415.
Hope is expressed that AP will be better than L. However, the quality of T's genius is in all his work.

*425.B "Novels and Novelists." *London (Quarterly) Review*, XVI (July), 281-313; Rptd. *Eclectic Magazine*, LIV (Sept.), 33-41; LIV (Oct.), 163-172.
T's work (VF and N) is discussed along with that of his

contemporaries. He is categorized as "an old Greek" of the cynic school. "VF is a remarkable book . . . ; but if we plunge beneath its sparkling surface, it is a dreary book. It gives the real, and . . . omits the ideal." In N there is a "better and brighter tone"—bitter irony is softened by pathos, and characters are not so absolutely good or bad.

*426.B *Athenaeum* (Nov. 30), pp. 718-720.
FG is a "brilliant picture of English life and manners, produced by honest reading." It will suit the prudish middle-class, since its tone is decorous and the morals are cued in when due, in spite of its "extremely wicked" charm.

427.B [Jewsbury, Geraldine]. *Athenaeum* (Dec. 7), p. 758.
L is "the sad failure of a man of genuine powers." "It is not sparkling bitter ale, but a deleterious beverage, neither good nor pleasant." T has abused his wide popularity. "The intense ingrained vulgarity" of L leaves the reader with a sense of "moral deterioration."

428.B *London Review*, III (Dec. 21), 780.
L refutes the notion that T is "a cruel and remorseless satirist." It indicates, rather, "a kindly generous nature, one who had felt for the sorrows of others."

1862

429.B "Satire and Satirists: Mr. Thackeray." *Eclectic Review*, CXV (Jan.), 1-16; Rptd. *Living Age*, LXXIII (April 26), 185-193.
Review of FG and L. T's traits as well as his place in literature are too well-fixed to be changed by these books. FG "is not history, but . . . historical costume." However, it is a "healthy book" in which T "lashes vice so heartily." His defect, though, is that he sees "a satiric side to all things." L shows some of the cynicism that was so prevalent in T's earliest work.

430.A Anderson, R. H. "Latter Day Fiction: Charles Reade." *Southern Literary Messenger*, XXXIV (Jan.), 10-17.
Bulwer's sentiment and Dickens' humor both tend to degenerate because of excesses, whereas "T's satire but deepens

from caustic wit to virtuous indignation." His characters are
more life-like than those of other novelists. *N*, for example,
is a book that is more than a satire or even a novel: "We
think of it as we think of Shakespeare's works."

431.B *Westminster Review*, N.S. XXI (Jan.), 289.
L would not have been revived at all if T were not its author.
It is the same old tune but with much inferior words. "Unless
he can compose something better than L, . . . he will be de-
posed from the place which he holds in popular estimation."

432.A [Curtis, George W.]. "Editor's Easy Chair." *Harper's Magazine*, XXIV (Feb.), 411-412.
A defense of L in response to No. 427 above. Although characters are low and repulsive, L's influence is not debasing.
T conveys moral meaning indirectly—by opposites.

433.A [Curtis, George W.]. "Editor's Easy Chair." *Harper's Magazine*, XXV (Aug.), 423-424.
The moral of AP is "simply that motives are mixed, that
people are not absolutely good nor irredeemably bad." "T's
range is limited. His genius is not opulent but it is profuse.
He does not create many types, but he endlessly illustrates
what he does create."

434.B [Chorley, Henry F.]. *Athenaeum* (Aug. 9), p. 174.
Review of AP. "T must look to his laurels. . . . The world
. . . will at last get tired of being led down alley after alley
of Vanity Fair." "It is not well put together" and T's perpetual interjections "tire and chill the interest."

435.B *John Bull*, XLII (Aug. 9), 508.
AP "will prove to be one of the works by which T will be
best known to posterity." Like all T's work, it will provide
"a rare memorial of us and our habits" from a moralist's point
of view. "Philip has a strongly marked nature of his own"
which is preferable to the "insipid" Clive Newcome or the
"gentishness" of Pendennis.

[436.]B *Literary Budget*, N.S. III (Aug. 9), 111; as quoted in Samuel A. Allibone, *Critical Dictionary of English Literature*. 3
vols. Philadelphia: Lippincott, 1871.

Review of AP. "Plot bad, characters good, moral dubious. It leaves Mr. T's reputation just exactly what it was, and ourselves in a state of placid indifference as to whether he writes more or not."

437.B [Bagehot, Walter]. *Spectator*, XXXV (Aug. 9), 885-886.
Review of AP. The theme is the relation of children to their parents, and, as usual, T's interest is in presenting "a sort of annotated picture." By such analysis he is able to provide a "minute anatomy" of that layer of life that lies just beneath the surface.

438.B *Saturday Review*, XIV (Aug. 23), 223-224.
Review of AP. At least T frankly admits to the practice of turning out a work even when he has nothing to say. His range is limited as well as his point of view. Thus, he turned to history, but it did not sell; and then the only recourse was to philosophize. In AP "we have much more of this sort of padding . . . than we ever had before." But "the bad book of a good author is never wholly bad."

439.B *Daily News*, Sept. 4, p. 2.
AP, "though tolerable . . . when . . . issued in monthly doses, is scarcely tolerable . . . altogether." T continually tells the reader how all will turn out, as well as lecturing and berating him. T's point of view in AP "takes in too cheerless an aspect of our common nature."

440.A [Curtis, George W.] "The Lounger." *Harper's Weekly*, VI (Sept. 20), 595.
AP (New York) "belongs in the same class as P and N" because of its style, characters, satire, and "simple, affectionate moralizing." "There is more meat in the nut he offers us than in many of a stronger and spicier flavor."

441.B *Westminster Review*, N.S. XXII (Oct.), 583.
AP, "if . . . not so good as we have a right to expect . . . , is much better . . . than most other authors could supply." Neither characters nor reflections are fresh, but both are well-presented. "It is almost too much to expect that . . . [a famous author] will be very solicitous about how he writes. . . . He considers fame to imply a large balance at his banker's."

[442.]B Williams, S. F. *Essays, Critical, Biographical and Miscellaneous.* London: Freeman, pp. 35-68.

443.A *Knickerbocker*, LX (Nov.), 463-464.
AP (New York) "is to a great extent a second-hand performance." "Nothing that a good writer produces is positively bad, but it is without that freshness, vigor, and life."
The old characters brought forth are wearisome.

444.A *Ladies Repository*, XXII (Nov.), 701.
Brief notice of AP (New York). " 'T's Abortions' have become a proverb. However, . . . in the sense of coining money
. . . , they are very far from being abortions. . . . T has the
remarkable facility of 'making a *little* go a great way.' . . . We
have fallen into the bad habit of not reading T any more."

445.B [Dallas, Eneas S.]. "Mr. Thackeray's Last Novel." *Times*,
Dec. 5, p. 6.
Review of AP. T is different from other novelists. His works
are half-sermons, and somehow leave the reader dissatisfied
at the end. Though the greatest living writer of idiomatic
English, he cannot resist a little pun, thereby spoiling an eloquent passage. "He has been too sensitive to criticism." Also,
too often "he appears to be so much above his trade." AP,
though melodramatic, is well done.

446.B *Saturday Review*, XIV (Dec. 27), 775-776.
Review of RP. "Although there is a certain amount of
thought in these essays it does not seem . . . particularly valuable." T's text always suggests the same sermons, "that the
world is a humbugging world." T's sensitivity to criticism,
particularly that of the *Saturday Review*, is questioned.

1863

447.A Davies, Samuel D. "Satirical Romance—Thackeray, Dickens,
Lever." *Southern Literary Messenger*, XXXVII (May), 298-
303.
A brief survey of satire and comedy in literature introduces
the three title authors as "at once philosophers, satirists, hu-

morists." Their works "differ essentially from every species of fictitious composition extant" in that there is little poetry or use of the pathetic. (Dickens is here an exception.) These writers show "a decided preference for the *common*, often bordering on the vulgar." This is not meant as a detraction from their merits, since "a common mind will degrade the loftiest theme, but a great and noble genius will dignify the meanest," as they in fact do.

448.B "Death of William Makepeace Thackeray." *Daily News*, Dec. 25, p. 4.
Obituary. Ever since P, critics charged T's writing with dwelling too much "on the dark and unlovely side of human character." E's "nobler tone" was an improvement perhaps suggested by public taste. It is N, however, that "revealed a deeper pathos than any . . . previous novels. . . . FG was not favorable to the display of . . . genial qualities." However, it must be said that T "uniformly employed his talents to make men better."

449.B "Death of Mr. Thackeray." *Morning Advertiser*, Dec. 25, p. 4.
Obituary. "T was not only in the prime of life, but in the zenith of his literary reputation."

450.B "Death of Mr. Thackeray." *Times*, Dec. 25, p. 7.
Obituary. T did not show his genius until VF. Though literary men prefer E because it is "the most finished of all his works," there is a "vigour" in VF and a "matured beauty" in N which make preference difficult. Except for Dickens, T ranked highest of English novelists; and as a writer of "pure idiomatic English," he had no peer.

*451.B [Forster, John]. "The Death of Mr. Thackeray." *Examiner*, (Dec. 26), pp. 817-818.
"He was sensitive to his sensitiveness. . . . Often he seemed . . . to be trifling or nervously obtruding himself into his story when he was but shrinking from the full discovery of his own simple intensity of feeling." N, more than any other book, sets cynicism aside and permits "discharge . . . of the whole, true mind of T."

1864

†452.A Reed, William B. *Haud Immemor*: A Few Personal Recollections of Mr. Thackeray. Philadelphia: Privately printed; Rptd. *Blackwood's Magazine*, CXI (June, 1872), 678-690; *Living Age*, CXIV (July 20, 1872), 157-165; *Eclectic Magazine*, LXXIX (Aug. 1872), 148-157.
Reed's home was T's house-of-call in Philadelphia. T's letters to Reed are reprinted. T "was free from that sentimental disease of 'Abolitionism.' "

453.A The *Age* (Richmond, Va.), I (Jan.), 74.
Memorial to "the wittiest English writer of the day." Specific praise for T's lecturing and for V.

454.A *Knickerbocker*, LXIII (Jan.), 90.
Review of RP (New York). T's eulogy of Washington Irving shows a departure from his "usual cynical style" and "chronic sneer." The other essays "read like long-drawn *asides* in his novels. They are for the most part dull reading, and would have failed to attract attention by the aid of their own merits."

455.B "Wm. Makepeace Thackeray." *Athenaeum* (Jan. 2), p. 20.
Obituary. E is "the most finished expression of T's powers as a scholar and an artist." But in all his work the same spirit exists, "a mixture of geniality and mistrust." Despite his having created the widest variety of characters in his work, not a single hero or heroine is likeable.

456.B Hannay, James. "The Late William Makepeace Thackeray." Edinburgh *Evening Courant*, Jan. 2, p. 3; Rptd. as *A Brief Memoir of the Late Mr. Thackeray*. Edinburgh: Oliver & Boyd.
Biographical sketch with critical comment. T was "essentially rather moralist and humourist,—thinker and wit,— than poet." Early works gave him reputation as satirist, though even then he showed a power for "representing tenderness" (GHD). EH is an example of his gift for re-creating the past. E shows a "richer imaginativeness" than other work.

457.B "Thackeray." *Reader*, III (Jan. 2), 3-4; Rptd. *Living Age*, LXXX (Feb. 6), 285-287.

Obituary. "T was characteristically a Victorian," and personally responsible for "that revival of a wholesome spirit of Realism."

458.B [Venables, George]. "Mr. Thackeray." *Saturday Review,* XVII (Jan. 2), 9-10; Rptd. *Living Age,* LXXX (Feb. 27), 413-415.
Eulogy of T, summarizing biographical facts, with some comment on the writings.

*459.B "Thackeray's Place in English Literature." *Spectator,* XXXVII (Jan. 2), 9-11; Rptd. *Living Age,* LXXX (Feb. 13), 325-328.
T cannot be categorized as satirist or humorist because his power was in combining "widely different elements, . . . tenderness of feeling, . . . masculine comprehensiveness, . . . [and] cynical fury." These permitted him to achieve the "wonderful shading of good into evil and strength into weakness." By developing beyond works such as YP and BL he was able to strike "the keynote of his genius,—the yearning to believe, the difficulty in believing, that there is anything deeper than human desires, anything which should limit our grief . . . at their habitual disappointment."

460.B "William Makepeace Thackeray." *Good Words,* V (Feb.), 192.
Memorial poem: "So loud he cried, a Snake in Beauty's bower."

461.B B[rooks], S[hirley]. *Illustrated London News,* XLIV (Jan. 9), 33-34; Rptd. *Living Age,* LXXX (Feb. 13), 290.
A personal memoir and biographical account of T. VF, P, E, and V comprise "the T Quadrilateral, which will defend his name and fame against all comers."

462.A [Mackenzie, Robert S.]. "William Makepeace Thackeray." *American Literary Gazette* (Phila.), II (Jan. 15), 204-208.
T approached, if he did not equal, Dickens' popularity, "but in his moral nature, as a writer, he was inferior." His humor was "sardonic and biting" rather than "genuine," and his "constructive power was small." His satire did not even have Fielding's "good nature." On the other hand he "carefully eschewed the indecorum" of *Tom Jones.*

463.A Sala, George A. "Thackeray." *Albion* (New York), XLII (Jan. 16), 29-30; Rptd. James G. Wilson, *Thackeray in the United States.* New York: Dodd, Mead, 1904, II, 22-32.
Eulogy and reminiscence. T's English was that of "an educated and travelled gentleman, . . . neither like a college Don . . . nor like a Saturday Reviewer in ignorant and supercilious conceit."

464.A 'N.' "Our London Correspondence." *American Literary Gazette* (Phila.), II (Feb. 1), 234-235.
With T's death, comparisons of him and other authors are out of place. T occupies his own "mountain-summit."

465.A *Atlantic Monthly*, XIII (Feb.), 261.
A review of RP (New York) is set aside in place of general tribute. "He was a man to be misunderstood continually; but his reward will be found a noble one, when the true story of his career is told."

466.B Dickens, Charles. "In Memoriam." *Cornhill*, IX (Feb.), 129-132; Rptd. *Living Age*, LXXX (March 5), 476-477; *Southern Literary Messenger*, XXXVIII (April), 244-246; *Eclectic Magazine*, LXII (May), 64-66; *Bibelot*, VII (Dec. 1901), 391-398.
A generous tribute to T's personal qualities, noting, however, his tendency "of undervaluing his art." DD is "much the best of all his works."

467.B H[oughto]n, [Lord]. [i.e., Richard Monckton Milnes]. "Historical Contrast." *Cornhill*, IX (Feb.), 133.
Memorial poem. "O gentle Censor of our age!/ . . . never wrath, except with Wrong./ Fielding without the manners dross."

468.B Trollope, Anthony. "W. M. Thackeray." *Cornhill*, IX (Feb.), 134-137; Rptd. *Eclectic Magazine*, LXII (May), 64-66.
Personal memoir. "He carried his heart-strings in a crystal case." E is "the first and finest novel in the English language. . . . Col. Newcome is the finest single character in English fiction."

469.B Hood, Thomas. "Thackeray and His Female Characters." *Englishwoman's Domestic Magazine*, N.S. VIII (Feb.), 157-164.
"He would have been considered a poet if he had not been a novelist." EH and FG are best examples of T's superb style. "His female characters had hearts and brains. . . . They are not dolls. . . . He appreciated women, and knew their influence and their sphere." (Description of some of the women in T's works follows.)

470.A *Ladies Repository*, XXIV (Feb.), 126-127.
RP (New York) is commended for its title, "but we have thus far read only the title-page."

*471.B K[ingsley], H[enry]. "Thackeray." *Macmillan's Magazine*, IX (Feb.), 356-363.
A memorial to T by way of critical praise for VF, "the most remarkable novel in the English language." T's use and creation of names is particularly praised.

472.B M[asson], D[avid]. "Thackeray." *Macmillan's Magazine*, IX (Feb.), 363-368.
T's work has "a more constant element of doctrine, a more distinct vein of personal philosophy," than that of most other novelists. E follows the imaginative line more. Dickens' and T's methods are compared. (See No. 148 above.)

473.B Michell, Nicholas. "William Makepeace Thackeray: In Memoriam." *New Monthly Magazine*, CXXX (Feb.), 154-155.
Poem: "Not cynical—he only lashed the times/ Sworn enemy to hypocritic art."/ . . . "Fielding of our day, and more than he."

*474.B [Brown, John, and Henry H. Lancaster]. "Thackeray." *North British Review*, XL (Feb.), 210-265; Rptd. *Living Age, LXXXI* (April 2), 3-34; John Brown, *Thackeray: His Literary Career.* Boston: Osgood, 1877; Henry H. Lancaster, *Essays and Reviews.* Edinburgh: Edmonston & Douglas, 1876, pp. 399-479; Rptd. in part as "Thackeray's Death." John Brown, *Horae Subsecivae.* 3 vols. Edinburgh: David Douglas, 1882, III, 177-194; *Bibelot*, VII (Dec. 1901), 399-419.

Biographical outline along with a critical account of T's writings. Even his first efforts show main interest: ridicule of the absurd. T was primarily a "satirist or humorist" rather than a novelist or story teller. The inconclusive endings of his works are indicative of this. Nevertheless, his characters are truly life-like and their fullness can only be matched by Jane Austen. P is "the gentlest and saddest of all his books." BL is the equal of *Jonathan Wild* in "sarcasm and remorseless irony." But T must be judged by all writing, not only novels. E, EH, and FG provide "the real essence of history." As an art critic T managed to re-create the painting while objectively criticizing it.

475.A *Southern Literary Messenger*, XXXVIII (Feb.), 121-122.
T's reputation with American readers is well-deserved. His delineation of American character was good, in spite of the "signal failure" of V. VF is the most widely acclaimed work, yet P is not really inferior. Neither T nor Dickens will suffer by comparison with the other when judged by posterity.

476.B Noel, Roden. "Thackeray." *Victoria Magazine*, II (Feb.), 347-348.
Poem: "He tore false trappings, . . ./Great satirist, great lover of the good."

477.B "The Eloges on Mr. Thackeray." *Spectator*, XXXVII (Feb. 6), 148-149.
Nos. 466, 468, and 471 above fail to do justice to T and point up the pitfalls which will face a biographer. T, as "a great national possession," must have a biography which will combine intellectual criticism with sympathetic appreciation of the man.

478.B Taylor, Theodore. [pseud. of John C. Hotten]. *Thackeray: The Humourist and the Man of Letters*. London: John C. Hotten; New York: Appleton.
Primarily an anecdotal biography, incorporating information printed in other such accounts, and also printing some of T's letters and youthful writings. Portrait presented is favorable, accenting T's integrity with his work and his personal generosity.

479.B "Thackerayana." *Reader*, III (Feb. 20), 225-228.
A biographical account, based on information in Nos. 474 and 478 above, the former of which is praised and the latter found acceptable.

480.B *Examiner* (Feb. 27), p. 135.
No. 478 above is premature, merely an outline of T's career, though its tone is basically sound. Period of T's work for *Examiner* is clarified.

481.A [Taylor, Bayard]. "William Makepeace Thackeray." *Atlantic Monthly*, XIII (March), 371-379; Rptd. *Critical Essays and Literary Notes*. New York: Putnam, 1880, pp. 134-154.
A personal memoir attesting to T's kindness, considerateness, and generosity. T never jeered at America.

*482.A [Whipple, Edwin P.]. "Thackeray." *Christian Examiner*, LXXVI (March), 211-222; Rptd. *Character and Characteristic Men*. Boston: Ticknor, Fields, 1867, pp. 197-217.
T was more a skeptic than a cynic. He was an observer with his eyes, "not a philosopher or poet. . . . He had no conception of causes and principles, no grasp of human nature as distinguished from the peculiarities of individuals." His inability to see meaning and purpose resulted in a skepticism "characteristic of the 'Bohemian' view of life." For example, though T had seen America, he could not understand the Civil War. However, his tenderness of heart, love of moral excellence, and ability to see through pretense saved him from the worst consequences of his skepticism. "The struggle between his feeling and his obstinate intellectual habit of minutely inspecting defects is obvious." But the final impression is "that life as he represents it is life not worth living."

483.A [Curtis, George W.]. "Editor's Easy Chair." *Harper's Magazine*, XXVIII (March), 563-564.
Eulogy and reminiscence of T. RP was "the simplest, pleasantest talk about smallest incidents, but full of general wisdom, tenderness and humility."

*484.B [Stephen, James F.]. "Mr. Thackeray." *Fraser's Magazine*, LXIX (April), 401-418; Rptd. *Eclectic Magazine*, LXII (June), 236-248.
To T's credit was the fact that he did not overrate himself

or the function of the novel. His air of pathos and lack of plot are the effects of a scrupulous modesty and factualness. S is a summary of T's early experience and writings. VF "is a sort of protest in behalf of the weak, the meek, the simple" —Becky a negative example of behavior. P is artistically inferior to VF and Pen's dependence on his wife is objectionable. "By the time he wrote N, T had . . . made friends with the world," but "there is something too luscious in Col. Newcome's love for his son, and in his dignity and meekness." E and V are "works of art simply" and are superior to other books, except perhaps BL.

*485.B [Simpson, Richard]. "Thackeray." *Home and Foreign Review*, IV (April), 476-511.
"The characters of T's novels are confessions and exhibitions of his own inner world," and because of this he excites personal sympathy. Similarly in his criticism, his ultimate aim is "to discover the soul that lurks within books and pictures." S is at the core of T's social criticism. "VF is the most objective work, because none of the characters in it are portraits of himself." T 's moral judgments are always couched in proverbs (i.e., popular attitudes). His failing in portraying good women is that he tries to present completed characters from the start rather than the development of their goodness. His own sadness about his wife led him to his "theory of mitigated affections." E gives indications that T once tried to be a Catholic.

486.B [Bagehot, Walter]. "Sterne and Thackeray." *National Review*, XVIII (April), 523-553; Rptd. *Literary Studies*. 2 vols. London: Longmans, Green, 1879, II, 106-145.
"T, like Sterne, looked at everything—at nature, at life, at art—from a *sensitive* aspect. His mind was . . . like a woman's mind." T's pre-occupation with snobs was due to an "irritable sensibility," which was at the base of his artistic character. In this he was more akin to Sterne than to Fielding who was a "reckless enjoyer."

487.A *North American Review*, XCVIII (April), 624-626.
RP shows T in the tradition of Steele. "The satire of T is the recoil of an exquisite sensibility from the harsh touch of life." T's full-characters and perfect style are contrasted to Dickens' "oddities" and "painfully mannered" writing.

488.A Grinnell, C. E. "A Word About Thackeray." *Yale Literary Magazine*, XXIX (April), 224-227.
Incorrect views of T result from the fact that satire is misunderstood, and thus it is not accepted as a form of moral criticism. The righteous prefer the cudgel to the whip or knife.

489.B "Thackeray." *Chambers's Journal*, XLI (April 30), 277-279.
Review of No. 478 above (a hurried and therefore unsatisfactory book) provides opportunity for giving a biographical sketch of T.

490.A *Eclectic Magazine*, LXII (May), 117-119.
A biographical sketch that focuses on the T-Dickens relationship. At close of T's life they were warm friends. In regard to literary preference, it is "a question as between two styles or theories of the art of prose fiction."

491.B "Thackeray the Preacher." *Eclectic Review*, CXIX (May), 562-593.
T was a "moralizing and tender" satirist, "not a *mere* cynic." Love of reality bred an "intolerance to all shamming and seeming. . . . Hence nearly all works . . . seem to be contained in S."

492.A [Curtis, George W.]. "Editor's Easy Chair." *Harper's Magazine*, XXVIII (May), 852-853.
"DD has the same sober air of historical reality which marks all T's novels." It seems also to be an attempt to correct the usual lack of incident.

493.B *Cornhill*, IX (June), 655-665.
Editorial note, following last part of DD, attempts to show— using T's notes—what the uncompleted DD would have been.

*494.B "Thackeray and Modern Fiction." *London (Quarterly) Review*, XXII (July), 375-408; Rptd. *Eclectic Magazine*, LXIII (Sept.), 38-56.
T's work is compared with the new crop of novels re the emphasis on moral qualities. T's books are "instructive illustrations" of how men repeat the same follies. S contains all the leading thoughts of succeeding works, in which "the moral tone . . . is always pure and elevating." Yet T (as well as

Dickens) made a false estimate of the value of Christian labors, and he was not impressed by clergymen. Perhaps his feelings came from observing "the unnatural severance between things sacred and secular."

495.B [Berdmore, Septimus]. "Thackeray." *Westminster Review*, N.S. XXVI (July), 172-185; Rptd. *A Scratch Team of Essays*. London: W. H. Allen, 1883, pp. 97-122.
T first gained public attention by the truth of his portrayals and his sense of justice. Gradually his work became artistically more perfect, but lost some of its moral purpose. T's critical spirit was tempered by social associations. His views of women, though failing to appeal to "the masses," "caught at the salient points which so strike the more educated and the more thin-skinned." Though apparently objective, T was a subjective writer, presenting his own feelings in both direct statement and dramatic action.

496.B "The Style of Balzac & Thackeray." *Dublin University Magazine*, LXIV (Dec.), 620-627; Rptd. *Living Age*, LXXXIV (Jan. 14, 1865), 51-58; *Eclectic Magazine*, LXIV (Feb. 1865), 229-236.
Balzac influenced T's style. Parallels in their careers are pointed out (e.g., both struggled for a period as bohemians); in their views of life; their use of same characters in different books; and their styles. The "same caustic vein of thought" and "the same pointed personal form of sentence" are discovered in two paragraphs of each writer.

497.B "William Makepeace Thackeray." *Leisure Hour*, XIII (Dec. 3), 774-780; XIII (Dec. 10), 790-791; Rptd. *Eclectic Magazine*, LXIV (March 1865), 340-348.
Largely a biographical account based on No. 456 above. Though T made some attempts in poetry and art, "he was hardly, in any high sense . . . , a poet. . . . To be a great artist was his never realized ambition." Even in later works there is much that is "jarring and repellent."

1865

498.B B[oyes], J[ohn] F. "A Memorial of Thackeray's School-Days." *Cornhill*, XI (Jan.), 118-128.
A schoolmate recalls T when 13-16 years old.

499.A *Atlantic Monthly*, XV (May), 639-640.
VF (New York) displays T's principal qualities though it does not include the full range of his genius. More than its successors, it has "freshness of feeling . . . and unity of aim." Old Osborne, "a representation of the most hateful phase of English character," is the most vivid and life-like of all characters. T's "perfect intellectual honesty" imparts a truth (though the view of life is narrow) to VF. (This edition seems to be the best made.)

500.A *Ladies Repository*, XXV (June), 380.
VF (New York) is a great work that needs no praise. This beautiful edition, though, is the finest yet.

501.A *Christian Examiner*, LXXIX (July), 154-155.
VF (New York) is an edition of quality fitting the dignity of T. "All T is in it." Few novels of greater fascination exist. All its elaborate details are carefully handled. It gathers together "an odious company" and "only Dobbin's foolish fidelity redeems the wretched story." Yet T forces us, in spite of ourselves, to a "considerable liking" for Becky.

1867

502.A *DeBow's Review*, N.S. III (April-May), 495.
P (New York) needs no comment other than notice of its availability in a new edition. "T was the priest of a higher art" than that of Dickens. The possibility of "intellectual enjoyment" in his work adds an interest that transcends plot and character.

503.A *DeBow's Review*, N.S. III (June), 604-605.
EH and FG (New York) provide a "delightful communion with the worthies of a past age."

504.A *Ladies Repository*, XXVII (July), 442.
P (New York) is part of a complete edition which is needed. "We esteem T a more unique writer than Dickens, and he was certainly more admirable as a man. His writings are satirical, but not bitter, incisive, but not cynical, . . . with a

vein of sympathy and sorrow for the very weaknesses he exposes."

505.A *Ladies Repository*, XXVII (Sept.), 571.
EH and FG (New York) "are first among the best of T's productions."

506.B Hannay, James. "Thackeray on Swift." *Temple Bar*, XXI (Oct.), 322-330; Rptd. *Living Age*, XCV (Nov. 9), 369-374. Comments on EH, wherein T's growing geniality and change from early satirical mood made him ungenerous to Swift while he overpraised Steele and Goldsmith.

1868

*507.B Hannay, James. "Studies on Thackeray." *Broadway*, 2nd ser. I (Sept.), 38-45; (Oct.), 138-144; (Nov.), 291-297; (Dec.), 324-329; Rptd. *Every Saturday*, VI (Oct. 3), 438-442; (Oct. 31), 553-556; (Nov. 28), 673-676; VII (Jan. 2, 1869), 10-13; *Studies on Thackeray*. London & New York: Routledge, 1869.
"T as a Novelist": Works "form a system of social philosophy" and the "range took in the whole society of England," which was subjected to a severe view because of T's faith in human nature. Even early work shows the mixture of good and bad in all characters.
"T as a Humorist & Satirist": Humor is both broad and fine (that of YP or a "subtle decorous irony"), and it is always moral and intellectual. S is his best satirical writing.
"T as a Critic & Essayist": A common-sense standard took the place of any cumbersome theory. In EH, though, the novelist usurped the critic's role. Sometimes T harped too much on one string, but his style was one of "easy familiarity . . . ; a peculiarly concise, yet very pregnant descriptiveness." He was a "Christian Horace."
"T as a Poet": "Rather a humorist who wrote poetry than a poet endowed with humour." He could express "everyday homely experience with a feeling which is truly poetic" but without the intensity "to sting the reader out of the sense of the common."

1869

508.A Barnes, James N. "Mr. Thackeray." *Lippincott's Magazine,*
III (Feb.), 150-161.
T's works, though great, may make us "sadder and wiser . . .
but not better, purer or happier." VF is his masterpiece. As
Candide embodies the principle of optimism, VF presents
"the pessimist view of life and its relations." T wrote VF to
shock the public in order to get noticed and to be read. "That
the world which it portrays is not the actual and real world
in which we live is too obvious for dispute." E's historical
aspects are excellent but they do not "compensate for the
shock to all natural feeling" which the story (the marriage)
imparts. T's decline began with N.

*509.B Sala, George A. "On a Certain Passage in *Vanity Fair*."
Belgravia, VIII (May), 345-355.
Verisimilitude is the highest achievement of fiction, and in
this VF excels all books. Thus, George Osborne's proposal
that Becky "fly" with him must be understood as a euphe-
mism for an assignation, rather than a plea for elopement,
which would be "grossly unreal."

510.B B., H. "On Thackeray's Place Among English Writers."
The *Month,* X (June), 513-530.
The question of T's place is deferred for posterity, and instead a defense is made of the faults often charged to T's
work: His intrusion into the story was to fulfill his role as a
teacher; lack of plot was to permit concentration on character; unlikeable characters exist because T did not extenuate
the truth.

511.A *Harper's Magazine,* XXXIX (Aug.), 452-455.
Dickens and T are without rivals among English novelists.
"One that reads to get a picture of Anglican life and man-
ners will find nothing so literally and exactly true as T."
VF, N, and V are announced in new (New York) editions.

512.B Mackay, William. "Thackeray and Sterne." *New Monthly
Magazine,* CXLV (Dec.), 628-644; CXLVI (Feb. 1870),
182-194; Rptd. (only first part) *Living Age,* CIV (Feb. 12,
1870), 387-396.

T was a preacher, and thus lectures were no surprise, but EH have little to commend them. T dwells on accidents rather than the essentials of Sterne's life and is unjust to him.

513.A *Nation*, IX (Dec. 9), 514.
C (New York) shows T's skill as an historical novelist and satirist, though it was hastily written in order to emphasize the moral. In 1840, C was needed "to satirize out of family reading the refined and philosophical highwayman. . . ."

1870

†514.A Griffin, Gilderoy W. *Studies in Literature*. Baltimore: H. C. Turnbull, pp. 104-108.
"VF presents a dreary picture of life, but . . . a true one." All T's characters are "natural and life-like," but Becky is beyond question his greatest portrayal.

515.B Bedingfield, Richard. "Recollections of Thackeray." *Cassell's Magazine*, N.S. I (March), 296-299; N.S. II (Sept.), 12-14, 28-30, 72-75, 108-110, 134-136, 230-232; Rptd. (first installment only) *Every Saturday*, IX (April 23), 259-260.
Personal memoir and commentary by T's cousin, who confirms T as a "real" contra "ideal" writer, skeptical of "the mighty passions which shake the world." A fine observer of manners and society, he nevertheless "had no ambition . . . to measure words with the very greatest writers." His cynicism was no more than a skin-deep theory.

516.B Mackay, William. "Thackeray's Later Manner." *New Monthly Magazine*, CXLVI (May), 579-584.
The preacher overcomes the artist in T's late work (e.g., AP). Especially bad are the intrusive estimates of a character which seem contradictory to the reader's own opinion.

517.A Hodder, George. "Recollections of William Makepeace Thackeray." *Harper's Magazine*, XLI (July), 261-269; see also *Memories of My Time*. London: Tinsley.
A personal memoir by T's secretary during the writing of FG.

1871

†518.A Reed, William B. *Among My Books.* New York: E. J.
Hale, "Novels—Defoe to Thackeray." pp. 182-198. "Thackeray Again." pp. 199-211.
T was Scott's only equal in re-creating history. His "historical romances," E and V, are proof of this and are perhaps his best work.
A personal memoir which praises T's forbearance in criticizing the U. S., and suggests his religious feeling and inclination towards Catholicism.

519.A Fields, James T. "Our Whispering Gallery." *Atlantic Monthly,* XXVII (Jan.), 125-137; Rptd. *Yesterdays with Authors.* Boston: Osgood, 1872, pp. 11-37.
Personal memoir and commentary on T's work: "Characters are . . . not so much *inventions* as *existences.*" T's great ability was to detect "the good or the vile wherever it existed."

*520.B "Two English Novelists: Dickens & Thackeray." *Dublin Review,* N.S. XVI (April), 315-350.
Dickens never matured as a writer; T did, and there was no decline in his powers. Both were preachers in the sense that all great novelists must be. But Dickens' false optimism and T's pessimism were mistaken views in the light of Christian-Catholic knowledge. T's scorn of vice, however, was at least the better of the two. T's work provides "intellectual satisfaction" and demands intellectual effort. In spite of artistry, BL is "an evil book." E, also, though without peer as historical fiction, is a painful and immoral book.

521.A "The Thinking of Thackeray." *Every Saturday,* X (April 8), 330-331.
T's originality lies in his fresh conception of old truths. "T is essentially a sceptic . . . whose tenderness of heart is at war with his experience of life." The drift of his intellect opposes his sentimentality. He is thus "the most popular novelist among the intellectual men and women of the generation," though "to the general reader T . . . is still a depressing influence." T's view leads to hopelessness, Dickens' to hope, but neither are really "thinkers."

1872

522.B Jerrold [William] Blanchard. *The Best of All Good Company*:
A Day with W. M. Thackeray. London: Houlston, pp. 315-
392.
Memoir of T, reprinting parts of Nos. 405, 456, and 468
above, and letters from Nos. 452 and 519 above, noting that
"his letters are a key to the kindlier and livelier side of his
character."

1873

523.B [Smith, George B.]. "The Works of Thackeray." *Edinburgh
Review*, CXXXVII (Jan.), 95-121; Rptd. *Living Age*, CXVI
(March 8), 579-593; *Every Saturday*, XIV (March 29),
340-348; *Eclectic Magazine*, LXXX (May), 513-528; *American Bibliopolist*, V (April), 64-66; V (May-June), 94-97;
V (July-Aug.), 132-137; VI (Jan.-Feb. 1874), 14-17; *Poets
and Novelists*. London: Smith, Elder, 1875, pp. 1-56.
"The key to T's work is to be found in his life" because he
relied on experience rather than imagination. Dickens was
his superior in invention. His principal defect is in drawing
pictures of manners, not men. E is "the most original of all
his books" and the best in "literary art." In N, "T rose to the
perfection of his art" and his moral instructiveness was
admirable.

524.A J., A. F. "The Novelist Thackeray." *Yale Literary Magazine*, XXXIX (Dec.), 128-139.
T's works are "essays upon social life," but it is questionable
whether he is representative of "the last cycle of fiction." He
wrote "beyond the rules," shunning sensationalism, and emphasizing character. The variety of his style is surprising,
considering the similarity of his themes. "As a moralist,
T is unexceptional."

1874

525.A Stoddard, Richard H. (ed.). *Anecdote Biographies of Thackeray and Dickens*. New York: Armstrong.
"Collection of the best papers . . . in an anecdotal sense."

Nos. 452, 474, 478, 517, and 522 above are quoted extensively.

526.A Lathrop, George P. "Growth of the Novel." *Atlantic Monthly*, XXXIII (June), 684-697.
"T . . . is far more dramatic, in the truest sense, than Dickens." Digression is his weakest feature. Much of his intrusion could be eliminated without destroying the "personal relation" with the reader, which also arises from his method of narration and the distinct personality in his style.

527.A Stoddard, Richard H. "William Makepeace Thackeray." *Harper's Magazine*, XLIX (Sept.), 533-549.
T's career was "unique" because so much of it was apparently wasted in teaching him what he could do best. "VF was an impersonal, objective book; P . . . was a personal one." E is T's masterpiece "as a work of art."

528.A B., H. R. "Thackeray's Estimate of Women." *Yale Literary Magazine*, XL (Nov.), 87-91.
T's "high and delicate . . . appreciation of the character of women" led him even to cease being a satirist in their portrayal. They are not extremes, but real persons—with all the petty faults. Lady Castlewood (E) is the noblest of his creations.

1875

529.B [Grego, Joseph]. *Thackerayana*. London: Chatto & Windus.
Selections from T's library (which was auctioned) are examined, providing a biographical glimpse at the relaxed side of T.

530.A [James, Henry]. "Thackerayana." *Nation*, XXI (Dec. 9), 376.
No. 529 above arouses curiosity for biographical detail without gratifying it. Though it does not seem true that T was always a good artist, nevertheless "there is no writer . . . from whom any chance quotation, to whom any chance allusion or reference, is more unfailingly delectable."

1876

531.B [Oliphant, Margaret]. "Mr. Thackeray's Sketches." *Black-wood's Magazine*, CXIX (Feb.), 232-243; Rptd. *Living Age*, CXXIX (April 8), 98-106.
Orphan of Pimlico; and Other Sketches, though revealing no new talent, reflect T's peaceful home and his closeness to his daughters. In his other works T's love of the paradoxes of human nature at first displeased readers, but "nobody has done such credit to the stupid gentleman with his good instincts and dull yet noble loyalty and steadfastness."

532.A Ripley, George, and Charles A. Dana (eds.). *American Cyclopaedia*. New York: Appleton, XV, 680-681.
VF gave T a reputation which, "though amply sustained, was hardly increased by any of his later works."

1877

533.A Lunt, George. "Recollections of Thackeray." *Harper's Magazine*, LIV (Jan.), 256-265.
N has too many "good" characters. Few are touched with vice at all. A character such as the Rev. Mr. Honeyman is satirized "from a ludicrous rather than a criminal point of view."

534.A Burpee, L. F. "Was Thackeray a Cynic?" *Yale Literary Magazine*, XLII (June), 393-396.
T was "certainly not a cynic." He is condemned because the vices he attacked are those which infected all society. His criticisms did not arise from spleen (like those of a cynic) but from the moral concern of a satirist.

1878

535.A Carey, Walter. "Hook, Thackeray, and Dickens." *Galaxy* (New York), XXV (Jan.), 31-43.
Hook was a sort of forerunner of T and Dickens in the novel of morals or social ethics. The influence seems stronger on T, because he served a longer apprenticeship. Main influence is *Gilbert Gurney*, though *Ramsbottom Letters* shows in YP.

1879

*536.B Trollope, Anthony. "Novel Reading." *Nineteenth Century,*
V (Jan.), 24-43.
(Article is of particular interest for the general comments on
the novel as a genre, which are later incorporated in *An Autobiography.* London: Blackwood, 1883). A brief summary
of the English novel illustrates the idea that novels must be
morally instructive in order to be taken seriously. Dickens'
popularity is wider than T's because he appeals to a "stratum
lower in education and wealth." E is T's greatest work and
an example of "good teaching." VF delights readers, but
does not satisfy them, because the characters are unattractive.

537.A Bibb, Grace C. "Thackeray." *Western,* N.S. V (Jan.), 1-17.
T, greater as a man than as a novelist, was a realist and hater
of all sham. Evil in his work seemingly triumphs often, but
this may be explained by his reliance on Christian justice—
a belief that only God is perfect.

538.B Pryme, Jane T., and Alicia Bayne. *Memorials of the Thackeray Family.* London: Privately printed.
An account of T's childhood, along with the family history,
by two kinswomen of T.

*539.B Trollope, Anthony. *Thackeray.* (English Men of Letters
Series.) London: Macmillan.
(Primarily a literary biography in which details of T's life
are incomplete and often inaccurate.) E is T's best work
as an artistic whole. BL is unrivalled for its continued irony
that is never irrelevant. P and N are chronicles rather than
novels and both are satirical in intention. Though VF is
both an interesting and a moral book, its severe truth made
people consider T a cynic. T's humorous and satiric light
verse will grow in estimation though he never took it seriously
himself. (A general impression of T's lack of artistic care is
likewise conveyed.)

540.B *Athenaeum* (June 14), pp. 749-750.
No. 539 above does not fill the need for a biography. It
rightly defends T from charge of cynicism, and points up the
great force of T's moral aim.

541.B Ward, T. H. *Academy*, XV (June 21), 533.
      Though No. 539 above does not credit T with the full and
      true effort that is in his work, Trollope's judgments are large-
      ly correct.

542.B "Contemporary Books." *Contemporary Review*, XXXV
      (July), 768-769.
      No. 539 above has "occasional touches of just criticism." T,
      though the greatest humorist of the century, was really a
      "survival" of the early eighteenth century, "placed at a dis-
      advantage in our much more self-conscious and speculative
      age." It is clear, though, that T was wholly lacking in rever-
      ence and faith. His writings are filled with "insolence towards
      human life."

543.A *Appleton's Journal*, N.S. VII (Aug.), 187-190.
      Agrees with the distinction made in No. 539 above that if
      satire is cynical then T was a cynic in his work, though not
      necessarily as a man.

544.A *Atlantic Monthly*, XLIV (Aug.), 267-268.
      Trollope was "unfit" to write No. 539 above. His criticism is
      "idle and valueless." For example, he completely misinter-
      prets T's idea of a snob.

545.A [Sedgwick, Arthur G.]. "Trollope's Thackeray." *Nation*,
      XXIX (Aug. 21), 127-128.
      No. 539 above fails in sympathy with its subject. It points out
      T's failings only to suggest Trollope's virtues. Its criticism
      is poor. Yellowplush, in fact, is quite different from a Mrs.
      Malaprop and serves different purposes also.

546.A Cooke, John E. "An Hour with Thackeray." *Appleton's
      Journal*, N.S. VII (Sept.), 248-254.
      T "was not a bitter cynic, but a person of the greatest gen-
      tleness and sweetness."

547.A *Lippincott's Magazine*, XXXIV (Sept.), 387-389.
      No. 539 above seems written with "indifference." It errs in
      playing down T's lectures, nor does it do justice to the effect

VF produced on the public. T's characters have always been as real to readers as personal acquaintances.

548.B "Thackeray." *Spectator*, LII (Sept. 6), 1130-1132.
No. 539 above is fairly done, though Trollope seems unaware how truly great T was. His amazing sense of reality is only matched by Jane Austen and sometimes George Eliot. E lacks "the fire and brilliancy of VF" but is "the most finished work of art." The ending is daring but undoubtedly right. "In one sense P is deepest of all novels since T strove to portray young men of his own day."

549.B Stephen, Leslie. "The Writings of W. M. Thackeray." *Works of W. M. Thackeray*. DeLuxe Ed. London: Smith, Elder, XXIV, 305-367.
T's work is viewed within the framework of literary history as well as examples of personal expression. Though autobiographical, T cannot be identified specifically with any of his creations. He reproduces, rather, the thoughts and sentiments of his own life. Literary influences are likewise apparent; for example, that of his "close and important" relation to Fielding. BL was produced when T's "intellectual power had reached its full development." No villain is "more supremely hateful and yet more thoroughly intelligible." T 's manner involves the spirit of irony, though not cynicism. VF is the closest "contact with the author's deepest nature"; whereas E gives free play to his imagination and style, "not consciously directed to any moral or social purpose."

550.B *Athenaeum* (Sept. 20), pp. 365-366.
"T's scorn of conventions did not go deep. . . . He was contented to accept a very conventional code of morality. . . . It is this mixture of half-hearted pessimism and real optimism that makes T so popular at present."

551.A [Faust, A. J.]. "William Makepeace Thackeray." *National Quarterly Review*, XXXIX (Oct.), 293-317.
Trollope was "unfitted" for writing No. 539 above. He particularly ignored that "strongly marked feature of T's character . . .—his reverence; and this seems the more singular as it is so distinctly traceable in all his higher writings."

1880

552.B Watt, James C. "William Makepeace Thackeray." *Great Novelists*. (Cabinet of Biography.) Edinburgh: Macniven & Wallace, pp. 97-159.
A digest of previous biographical and critical pieces.

553.A Sturgis, Russell. "Thackeray As a Draughtsman." *Scribner's Monthly*, XX (June), 256-274.
32 cuts of T's own drawings are printed with commentary, showing that he had "a novelist's feeling for character" but that the sketches do not display the skill of a graphic illustrator.

1881

*554.A Nadal, Ehrman S. "Thackeray's Relations to English Society." *Scribner's Monthly*, XXI (Feb.), 535-543; Rptd. *Essays At Home and Elsewhere*. London: Macmillan, 1882, pp. 86-112.
T was more of a social critic than an artist. Much of his concern about snobbery, his self-depreciation and self-doubt, and his humor itself spring from the uncertain social status allotted to him by English society—"the most egotistical in the world." (See No. 555 below.)

*555.A [Brownell, William C.]. "Recent Discoveries Concerning Thackeray." *Nation*, XXXII (Jan. 27), 56-57.
T "discovered snobbishness to be an integral element of human nature," and expressed a distinct dislike of its meanness, though he readily admitted to some of the general tendencies in himself. No. 554 above errs, perhaps from national prejudice, in thinking that the snob is a particularly English institution; or that T's interest grew from "a fellow feeling of sycophancy."

556.B "Thackeray As a Poet." *Temple Bar*, LXI (April), 469-475; Rptd. *Potter's American Monthly*, XVI (June), 517-520; *Eclectic Magazine*, XCVII (July), 96-100.
T "must be assigned a high place among the poets of the century" if poetry is understood as "a criticism of life" and "the

application of ideas to life." He also merits consideration as a writer of *vers de société*.

557.B [Henley, William E.] *Athenaeum* (Nov. 12), pp. 623-624; Rptd. *Eclectic Magazine*, XCIX (July 1882), 119-122; Rptd. (with slight changes) *Views & Reviews: Essays in Appreciation*. New York: Scribner, 1890, pp. 9-19.
"He may have been a little man, but . . . he was a great writer; he may have been a faulty novelist, but he was a fine artist in words. . . . T's morality is that of a highly respectable British cynic."

1882

558.A Williams, Alfred M. "A Real Barry Lyndon." *Catholic World*, XXXVI (Nov.), 194-204.
T's ability as an historical novelist is discussed, with praise especially for C and BL where he shows "sympathy and understanding of the essential elements of Irish nature." The memoirs of William "Tiger" Roche undoubtedly served as source material for BL.

1883

559.A Henry, Maria L. "The Morality of Thackeray and of George Eliot." *Atlantic Monthly*, LI (Feb.), 243-248.
Works of both authors create the "feeling of sadness and discouragement." T's mistrust of human nature and his stoicism toward the evils in life betray a "lack of religion," just as the "modern humanitarianism" of George Eliot does. Because T was not a bitter cynic, his doctrine is the more dangerous because more palatable. It encourages a sort of "content with low achievement."

560.A Vernon, Henry J. "Where Colonel Newcome Died." *Peterson's Magazine* (Phila.) LXXXIV (July), 29-34.
The actual London setting of the death of the most pathetic personage in English fiction is described.

561.A Faust, A. J. "William M. Thackeray." *American Catholic Quarterly*, VIII (Oct.), 597-627.

The idea that T's views are harmful is completely false. Nor was T's thinking "turbid and confused" (as No. 554 above would claim). He did not aim his satire at a special class but "at things wrong in and of themselves." "His realism is that of a perfectly sustained probability." In all his work is found "a wide toleration of the feelings and opinions of others." Mme. de Florac's depiction illustrates "his respectful attitude towards the Catholic Church," just as the whole of N "has yet no shaft to wound any sincerely Christian heart."

562.A Rideing, William H. "In the Footsteps of Thackeray." *Century*, XXVI (Oct.), 830-844.
Fictional settings are reconstructed with reference to the real London, although it is stated that T's sense-of-place is less well-developed than that of Dickens. (See No. 564 below.)

1884

563.B Traill, Henry D. "Sterne and Thackeray." *The New Lucian*. London: Chapman & Hall, pp. 237-253.
Satirical dialogue in which issues of sentiment, cynicism, and style are debated. T is shown to have wrongly judged Sterne.

564.A Rideing, William H. "Thackeray in London." *Critic*, IV (April 19), 181-182; IV (April 26), 193-194; substantially incorporated (along with No. 562 above) in *Thackeray's London*. London: J. W. Jarvis, 1885.
Referring to No. 562 above and certain criticisms of it, Rideing reasserts that T, unlike Dickens, does not "fill us with suggestiveness" for every nook of London. "T's method was to merely sketch a background and to let his figures fill the picture." His limitation is in part due to his abhorrence of low-life.

565.B Cook, Dutton. "Thackeray and the Theatre." *Longman's Magazine*, IV (Aug.), 409-423; Rptd. *Critic*, V (Aug. 16), 80-82; V (Aug. 23), 92-93; *Choice Literature*, IV (Sept.), 214-221.
T was not a dramatist, but his knowledge of actors and the theatre was used in the novels. He was a constant playgoer and wrote much sound dramatic criticism.

566.B. "Thackeray and Romanticism." *Saturday Review*, LVIII (Oct. 18), 473-474; Rptd. *Critic*, XI (Aug. 27, 1887), 107-108.

A restatement of an observation made in No. 549 above, regarding T as a "British Philistine" (especially in his youth), that is based on his opinions of the French Romantic movement and such writers as Balzac, Hugo, and Sand.

1885

567.A Mason, Edward T. *Personal Traits of British Authors*. Vol. IV. New York: Scribner, pp. 267-314.

A compilation of biographical miscellany from nearly all previous articles and books. (Sources are cited.)

568.B *Athenaeum* (Oct. 17), pp. 497-498; Rptd. *Critic*, VII (Nov. 7), 225-226.

Miscellaneous Essays, Sketches, and Reviews shows the early-achieved polish of T's style in distinction to that of Dickens, but likewise indicates his limitation, even at the start, to the "gentleman's interest."

569.B "Thackeray's Miscellaneous Essays." *Saturday Review*, LX (Oct. 17), 514-515.

T left nothing that is without value to the student of style, though many of the early topical essays make no real impression any longer.

570.A Young, Ephraim. "Thackeray as an Art-Critic." *Atlantic Monthly*, LVI (Nov.), 685-693.

An examination of the "Titmarsh" articles (1838-1839) on painters and painting, wherein T pleaded for "sincerity, naturalness, and truthfulness in art."

1886

571.B Dawson, George. "William Makepeace Thackeray." *Biographical Lectures*. London: Kegan Paul: Trench, pp. 438-450.

T "is thoroughly and intensely in his books," which indicate a "cultivated . . . [and] a very generous man." In his hands the novel became the "truest way of representing the spirit of the time."

*572.A Johnston, Richard M. "The Extremity of Satire." *Catholic World*, XLII (Feb.), 685-694.
The faculty for fiction writing which God gave to some must be used only for "benign purposes." Satire is a dangerous method of instruction because the reader is led to admire what is "seductive and evil." This is especially true in VF. There, also, certain character relationships (paralleled in E) are "unnatural" and "revolting."

573.B Wilson, Henry S. "Madame de Florac." *Gentleman's Magazine*, CCLX (June), 561-576.
By means of a glowing account of Mme. de Florac (N), an attempt is made to demonstrate T's concern for "character" as opposed to reliance on "mere plot."

574.A Guiney, Louise I. "Concerning Thackeray." *Critic*, VIII (June 19), 301-302.
A humorous letter to the dead Dickens, pointedly showing his faults of both character and art, and doing the same collaterally for T. The perpetual debate upon one or the other's ascendancy is summed up. Their fate in the afterlife is to be "named, associated, and discussed out of all patience, in perpetual conjunction."

1887

Entries for this year are arranged chronologically, as usual, with the exception that the notices of the Brookfield letters are grouped together following No. 575 below.

575.B Dolman, Frederick. "Was Thackeray a Cynic?" *Time*, 2nd ser. VI (Aug.), 188-195.
Only careless reading gives rise to the impression that T was a cynic. He was the great satirist of the nineteenth century because he had so much faith in human nature. The good that is found even in his bad people is proof. The high-life he depicted, though limiting his scope, actually was a better object for satire, especially since it seems probable that he considered a landed aristocracy more of an evil than a good.

Notices of the Brookfield Letters

The notices below are of the collection of T letters as they appeared in *Scribner's Magazine*, I (April) through II (September); or in one of the book editions: Mrs. Jane O. Brookfield (ed.). *A Collection of Letters of W. M. Thackeray 1847-1855*. New York: Scribner, 1887; London: Smith, Elder, 1887.

Generally, these reviews note the amiable and generous character of T which emerges from the correspondence. The comments offered with the entries below, therefore, are only those which add to this observation or differ from it.

576.B "Unpublished Letters of Thackeray." *Athenaeum* (March 26), pp. 417-418; (April 16), p. 514; (May 2), p. 674; (June 18), p. 800; (July 23), pp. 116-117; (Aug. 20), pp. 244-245; (Sept. 24), p. 404; (Oct. 29), p. 563.
The letters reveal the autobiographical element in T's work; e.g., the personal thoughts and ideas in P. They deserve better editing, with annotation where necessary. The publishers are urged to enlarge the collection with the T letters that others may have.

577.B "Mr. Thackeray's Letters." *Saturday Review*, LXIII (April 2), 480.
Mrs. Brookfield is thanked for publishing.

578.B "Thackeray's Letters." *Spectator*, LX (April 2), 459-460.
Complaint against the unvarying satirical tone in the first installment (*Scribner's*, April), and also that they "are not . . . so good . . . as his greater writings would lead us to expect."

579.A Hawthorne, Julian. *Bookmart*, IV (May), 496.
"The greatest of English novelists . . . goes on being a great novelist in these private communications." They contain "the familiar old irony."

580.B "Letters of Thackeray." *Saturday Review*, LXIV (Sept. 17), 404-405.
The spirit of the letters is concordant with that of the novels. The cautious editing of "the questionable personal elements" is approved.

581.A Bunner, Henry C. "On Reading Certain Published Letters of William Makepeace Thackeray." *Scribner's Magazine*, II (Oct.), 448.
Poem: Before these letters were available, only a few ". . . had grace/to see, past all misjudgment: his true heart."

582.B *Blackwood's Magazine*, CXLII (Nov.), 698-704.
Dickens' letters show little personal identity and charm in contrast to T's.

583.A *Princeton Review*, LXII (Nov.), 395-396.
The judgment of T as a cynic is now reversed.

584.A. "Thackeray's Letters." *Atlantic Monthly*, LX (Dec.), 853-855.
"The identity of the man and the author" confirms T's "sincerity."

585.A Johnson, Edward G. "Thackeray's Letters." *Dial*, VIII (Dec.), 181-182.
T's generous praise of Dickens is noted. The style is a "standard of epistolary excellence."

586.B "Thackeray's Letters." *Spectator*, LX (Dec. 24), 1790-1791.
They reveal T as often bowed by "the sadness and vanity of life."

1888

Entries for this year are arranged chronologically, as usual, with the exception that the notices of the Brookfield letters are grouped together before other entries.

Notices of the Brookfield Letters (cont.)

587.B Sichel, Walter. "Thackeray's Letters." *Time*, 2nd ser. VII (Jan.), 19-25; Rptd. *Living Age*, CLXXVI (Feb. 18), 439-443.
"T attracts . . . with something of a school-boy freshness"; "an honest, high-spirited love of frolic pervades the deep and keen observation."

588.A Repplier, Agnes. "Letters of Thackeray." *Catholic World,* XLVI (Feb.), 593-602.
Writing for a living must have depressed T at the start. Later he seems "singularly sensitive to the vulgar publicity that attends a successful man of letters." T's generous praise of Dickens is noted.

589.B. Francis, M. E. "Thackeray's Letters." *Irish Monthly Magazine,* XVI (Feb.), 84-92.
T's personal troubles prevented him from believing in earthly bliss.

590.B Lang, Andrew. "Thackeray." *Good Words,* XXIX (Jan.), 14-19; Rptd. *Essays in Little.* New York: Scribner, 1891, pp. 103-117.
T, "humorist whose mirth springs from his melancholy," has, more than any English writer, a "poetic quality" in his inimitable style. Because he portrays human nature and conduct with such complete verisimilitude, we can hardly complain that he did not write "a complete good story."

591.B Forster, Joseph. "William Makepeace Thackeray." *London Society,* LIII (Feb.), 143-152.
An "attempt to destroy the vulgar and utterly erroneous opinion many people have of his cynicism."

592.A Stevenson, Robert L. "Some Gentlemen in Fiction." *Scribner's Magazine,* III (June), 764-768.
Though T himself "scarce appeals to us as the ideal gentleman" (because of his snobbery), he certainly, more than most writers, was able to depict the type. Some are petty and some are tainted with vulgarity, but gentlemen nevertheless. And if ever the art of being a gentleman is forgotten, it can be relearned from a study of Colonel Newcome.

593.B Merivale, Herman C. "About Two Great Novelists." *Temple Bar,* LXXXIII (June), 188-204; Rptd. *Living Age,* CLXXVIII (July 21), 159-169; *Eclectic Magazine,* CXI (Aug.), 231-241; *Bookmart,* VI (Aug.), 130-142.
Biographical scraps about T and Dickens. T's ability to lecture was paralleled by his ability "to talk to you . . . familiarly

in pen-and-ink." A main impression of his work, in which
the art is largely concealed, is "massiveness." T had the
spirit of a poet, and it showed even in his prose.

594.B Pollock, Walter H. *Encyclopedia Britannica.* 9th ed.
"The force and variety of his genius and art will always hold
for him a place as one of the greatest of English novelists
and essayists." In VF there are no minor figures who are in-
completely or inconsistently depicted, and Becky is an example of a "supreme art . . . that makes the reader understand and feel her attractiveness, though he knows her ex-
traordinary evil qualities."

1889

595.B Johnson, Charles P. "An Early Scrap-Book of W. M. Thackeray." *Athenaeum* (April 6), pp. 445-446.
The drawings in T's early sketch book (1841) might be fore-
runners of later character creations.

596.B "The Prototypes of Thackeray's Characters." *Temple Bar,*
LXXXVI (May), 103-110; Rptd. *Living Age,* CLXXXI
(June 15), 694-699; *Eclectic Magazine,* CXIII (July), 1-5.
An attempt to relate some of T's characters to his real-life
acquaintances. Also, the death scene of the old trapper in
The Prairie (Cooper) is identified as the source for T's treat-
ment of Colonel Newcome's death when he rises and says,
"*Adsum.*"

*597.B Gonner, Edward C. K. "Thackeray's Genealogies." *Time,*
3rd ser. I (May), 501-508; (June), 603-610.
T develops characters with details that include not only habits and dress but dates of birthdays and weddings, as well as
exact family connections. Thus genealogical tables are made
up for the fictional families of Newcomes, Warringtons, and
Esmonds.

598.A Lang, Andrew. "Thackeray's London." *Lost Leaders.* New
York: Longmans, Green, pp. 166-172.
Contrary to the idea (in No. 564 above) that readers will

forget the settings of T's fiction, Lang believes that T's fictional London is as real and as durable as that of Dickens.

599.A *Critic*, XV (July 13), 21-22.

No. 596 above is criticized for its concern with the prototypes of fictional characters; however, much of the information is restated.

1890

†600.B Church, W. E. *W. M. Thackeray As an Artist and Art Critic*. n.p., n.d.
"T's genius as an artist is best shown in caricature." But his formal training in art did serve to make him a competent art critic.

601.B Wilson, Henry S. "Colonel Newcome." *Gentleman's Magazine*, CCLXVIII (May), 497-509.
The Colonel's fine traits of character are lauded with the object of showing T's concern for "character" as opposed to "mere plot."

602.B Ritchie, Anne T. "Chapters from Some Unwritten Memoirs."
Macmillan's Magazine, LXII (July), 189-192; (Aug.), 252-256; LXIII (Dec.), 112-118; LXIII (Feb. 1891), 249-253; (April 1891), 424-428; LXVI (May 1892), 17-22; (Aug. 1892), 265-270; (Sept. 1892), 344-349; LXVIII (July 1893), 190-196; LXIX (April 1894), 443-450; LXX (Oct. 1894), 429-434; Rptd. *Living Age*, CLXXXVI (Aug. 23), 493-496; (Sept. 20), 745-748; CLXXXVIII (Jan. 3, 1891), 120-125; (March 7, 1891), 633-637; CLXXXIX (May 2, 1891), 295-298; CXCIII (June 25, 1892), 819-824; CXCV (Oct. 8, 1892), 108-113; (Oct. 22, 1892), 249-254; CXCVIII (Sept. 2, 1893), 549-555; CCI (April 28, 1894), 226-233; CCIII (Dec. 1, 1894), 548-553.
Chapters from Some Memoirs. London: Macmillan, 1894; New York: Harper, 1895.
Charm and perception are evident in these personal glimpses of T by his daughter, but they do not provide biographical detail.

1891

603.B Merivale, Herman C. and Frank T. Marzials. *Life of W. M. Thackeray.* London: Walter Scott. The first attempt at a full biography, but without access to private documents. Random critical comments are offered, but without a central point of view. E is T's perfection; RP is the "flower of his later works." Because of style T is "the first English prose classic of this century." He was a bookish writer, not only because of frequent allusions, but also for his portraits of literary men. Though he intruded authorial comment in his works, it did not hinder the living quality of his characters.

604.B *Athenaeum* (Feb. 14), pp. 209-210. Despite No. 603 above, "the life of T worthy of the man has still to be written."

605.B "Was Thackeray Most Satirist or Novelist?" *Spectator*, LXVI (Feb. 28), 303-304. A distinction is made between the "satirist's art" and the "novelist's art," the latter dealing with the "wholesome" and "all that is good and commonplace." Thus, T became a great satirist but not a great novelist.

606.B Johnson, Lionel. *Academy*, XXXIX (March 7), 226-227. No. 603 above is reviewed and its notion that a satirist and a humorist are contradictory roles is attacked. T was both. T's use of intrusive comments in the novels is also defended.

607.B Lang, Andrew. "Thackeray and His Biographers." *Longman's Magazine*, XVII (April), 673-678; Rptd. *Living Age*, CXC (July 4), 44-46. Biographies and reminiscences of T published to date are examined for their inadequacies. They are either adulatory or slanderous, or merely anecdotal.

608.B Ritchie, Anne T. "Thackeray and His Biographers." *Illustrated London News*, XCVIII (June 20), 811. A sharply critical review of all the biographies published, citing their limited viewpoints and inability to understand the whole man, as well as their intrusion on the privacy of the family circle.

609.B Layard, George S. "Thackeray's Portraits of Himself." *Murray's Magazine*, X (Aug.), 229-236; Rptd. *Living Age*, CXCII (Jan. 9, 1892), 125-128.
The many self-portraits and self-caricatures which T drew for the magazines and which adorned the margins of his own work are mentioned briefly.

1892

610.B Davies, Gerald S. "Thackeray as Carthusian." *Greyfriar*, II (April), 61-67.
T's schooldays at Charterhouse (1822-1828), with reproductions of some of T's early drawings.

611.A Hutson, Charles W. "The Morality of Thackeray's Art." *Education*, XII (May), 531-537.
"The highest morality is truth" and T's art is "so true to nature" that it embodies a "living morality." Unfortunately most of his work is not tempered by "Cervantic humor." Only when he produces the contrast of good and evil characters (as in P, E, and N) does he show his best moral qualities.

612.A Mallock, William H. "Are Scott, Dickens, and Thackeray Obsolete?" *Forum*, XIV (Dec.), 503-513.
The novel resists obsolescence more than other forms. Certain writers (T included) "in describing their own times perpetuate the social atmosphere in which they are to be understood." However, the social range of T's characters was more limited than those of Scott or Dickens, and thus he has now (as always) a more restricted group of readers, though among these interest is not diminishing.

1893

613.B Fraser, William A. *Hic et Ubique*. London: Sampson Low, Marston, pp. 147-179 and *passim*.
A personal memoir, including Fraser's initial reaction to VF, which he found deserving to be placed beside Shakespeare and the Bible. Other comments: EH merely held great men up to scorn. T's use of the same characters in different novels is bad.

614.AB Crowe, Eyre. *With Thackeray in America.* New York:
Scribner; London: Cassell.
Crowe accompanied T "as his factotum and amanuensis" on
his lecturing trip in the U.S. (1852-1853). Though of biographical interest, the book is more a chronicle of Crowe's
travels while on T's business. Impressions of persons and
places are accompanied by sketches.

615.B Irvine, John W. "A Study for Colonel Newcome." *Nineteenth Century*, XXXIV (Oct.), 584-595; Rptd. *Living Age*,
CXCIX (Dec. 2), 563-571; *Eclectic Magazine*, CXXI
(Nov.), 645-652.
A personal reminiscence with the purpose of describing T's
visit to Charterhouse, where he met a pensioner who served
as a partial model for the Colonel.

616.B Vizetelly, Henry. *Glances Back Through Seventy Years.* 2
vols. London: Kegan Paul, Trench, Trubner, I, 281-301
and *passim*.
A familiar of T's from 1845 on, the writer provides biographical and anecdotal material.

1894

617.B Fiennes, Gerard. "Some Notes Upon Thackeray." *New Review*, X (March), 337-345; (April), 499-506.
Some sketches drawn by T are presented with notes. As
clearly as VF or P, they indicate T's gift for close observation,
his appreciation of the ridiculous, and the undercurrent of sadness or bitterness. DD would have been his finest work because the satirical strain had mellowed.

618.B Edwards, Amelia B. "The Art of the Novelist." *Contemporary Review*, LXVI (Aug.), 225-242.
T's works, along with those of Dickens and Trollope, are
representative of "the historical novel of contemporary English life." T reads men through and through. He is "the
greatest master of fiction the world has seen." Rather than
cynicism, it is "infinite sympathy with all that is best" which
his work displays. E is his masterpiece.

619.A Harrison, Frederic. "Thackeray's Place in Literature." *Forum*, XVIII (Nov.), 326-338; Rptd. *Studies in Early Victorian Literature*. London-New York: E. Arnold [1895], pp. 107-127.
None of T's work is utterly worthless, perhaps if only because of his style which places him "among the very greatest masters of English prose." But "the substance and effective value of his great books" do not win him an equal place. There is a bitter taste after VF. Nor did T portray "women to love and to honour." E has the qualities of a great book "except its artificial form . . . and its unsavoury plot." T's place in literature will be determined by VF.

620.B "Thackeray's Place in Literature." *Saturday Review*, LXXVIII (Nov. 24), 553-555.
No. 619 above praises T's minor achievements, having done T less than justice in other respects. Harrison is Mrs. Grundy's advocate when he criticizes VF as ungenial. Actually it is "the greatest prose work in English Literature" with only *Don Quixote* as its superior in all literature.

1895

621.B Saintsbury, George. "Thackeray." *Corrected Impressions*. London: Heinemann, pp. 1-20.
The mainspring of T's genius is his conception and projection of character; the greatest fault is construction. His complete works have a uniformity rarely found. It was a scene in V that made the writer a T admirer, and "a favorable impression of him, once reached, . . . is never more to be corrected or altered."

622.A Boyesen, Hjalmar H. "The Great Realists and the Empty Story-Tellers." *Forum*, XVIII (Feb.), 724-731.
Children especially should read realists like T, George Eliot, and Tolstoy rather than the writers of romances, in order to secure "as intimate an acquaintance as possible with one's own environment." T's work has the power to kindle a spark of self-criticism in the reader.

623.B "Thackeray's Legal Career." *Law Times*, XCVIII (March 23), 496-497; Rptd. *Green Bag*, VII (Aug.), 372-373.
An account of T's tenuous connection with law. It was well he did not practice, since legal matters might have tended "to blunt the finer and more sensitive parts of his nature."

*624.B Jack, Adolphus A. *Thackeray: A Study*. London: Macmillan.
All of T's work is examined and seen as falling into three periods: that before VF; VF itself, which utilized all the techniques and attitudes of earlier work; and finally P and its successors. There was a continuous development of T, especially after P, in which he adopted a more humane manner, which ripened in E and N. Not lack of a hero, but lack of heroic qualities differentiates VF. It is a book that seems true while being read, but afterwards is seen as "one entire impossibility." In P, T really began to present "real living men and women." As a critic T's judgments are too black and white (e.g., EH). Overall, he must be viewed more as a preacher than artist. The complete canon, rather than a single book, will secure his place as a "classic."

625.B M., A. "An Estimate of Thackeray." *Bookman*, VIII (May), 50.
No. 624 above lacks sympathy with T's kind of exuberant energy which in fact produced many lesser things (along with greater). For these Jack's judgments are too solemn and severe.

*626.A Howells, William D. "Thackeray." *My Literary Passions*. New York: Harper, pp. 129-138 and *passim*.
T was one of the "very great" who for a time took hold of Howells' affection and imagination (*ca.* 1850). At present most of the attractions have been dulled. The once realistic novels seem "overcolored" and caricatured, and T's philosophy unsubstantial. VF seems the poorest of T's work, P the best. BL displays T's ironic talents at their best. The love affair in E is an "unpleasant and preposterous affair."

627.B "Thackeray's London." *Temple Bar*, CV (July), 422-432; Rptd. *Living Age*, CCVI (Aug. 17), 412-419.
Some associations of London localities with T and his characters.

628.A Fisher, Mary. *Twenty Five Letters on English Authors.* Chicago: S. C. Griggs, pp. 374-378.
Only an improper reading of T yields the impression that he was a cynic. His work was "a new and healthy force in literature, a powerful antidote against the Bulwer school." VF, once rejected, "is now a recognized classic."

629.B Marzials, Frank T. *Academy,* XLVIII (Sept. 14), 201.
No. 624 above too often "expects from T what T did not propose to give," e.g., that FG should be connected history. Nor does Jack appreciate T's humor.

630.B Lilly, William S. "The Humourist as Philosopher: Thackeray." *Four English Humourists of the Nineteenth Century.* London: John Murray, pp. 37-72.
T is defended as a philosopher against Taine's criticism that he looks upon passions as moral qualities rather than as poetic forms. Stress is laid on the novelist's need to be concerned with "perceptions of right and wrong," and though T lacked Balzac's genius and talent, he is like him in his "gift of moral second sight." T's philosophy in essence is Kantian.

631.A Hubbard, Elbert. "W. M. Thackeray." *Little Journeys to the Homes of Good Men and Great.* New York-London: Putnam, pp. 231-257.
T's witty humor was often too deep for the reader, thus the charges of cynicism and pessimism were made. In Becky T presented "some of his own weak points and then lashed them with scorn."

1896

632.A Grange, A. M. "Catholicism in Thackeray and Dickens." *American Catholic Quarterly,* XXI (Jan.), 142-154.
Dickens' best example of his Catholicism is "A Christmas Carol." He always treats sin and repentance from a Catholic viewpoint. Both men wrote respectfully of the Catholic Church. Even in BL, "the most unredeemable story that T ever wrote," he refrains from an attack on the Church. His "fiercest sneer is reserved for his own church." T's hypocrites are not Catholics. Father Holt (E) is "at once fascinating and to some extent sincere." Neither man, however, could grasp the Catholic idea of womanhood.

633.B Fisher, W. E. G. "The Real Barry Lyndon." *English Illustrated Magazine*, XIV (March), 625-628.
Casanova's self-portrait in his memoirs served as the source for BL, although certain candid admissions were wisely omitted.

634.A Linton, E[lizabeth] Lynn. "Landor, Dickens, Thackeray." *Bookman* (New York), III (April), 125-133; Rptd. *My Literary Life*. London: Hodder & Stoughton, 1899.
T and Dickens are examples of the "divorcement of intellect and character." T's writing is stern and critical, though he was generous and free of suspicion; whereas Dickens, a harsh and over-cautious man, wrote very humanely.

635.A Young, Truman P. "Mr. Roundabout—His Papers." *Yale Literary Magazine*, LI (June), 377-380.
An appreciation of T the writer and the man as revealed through RP.

636.A "Who Was the Imitator, Dickens or Thackeray?" *Atlantic Monthly*, LXXVIII (July), 139-141.
An examination of similarities in P and *David Copperfield* (especially the Steerforth-Emily episode in comparison with Pen and Fanny Bolton), indicating that T was influenced by Dickens, though he produced something distinct and with deeper insight.

637.A Hyde, George M. "The Cynicism of Thackeray and the Sadness of George Eliot." *Dial*, XXI (July), 9-10.
It is wrong to categorize the entire canon of either writer by the qualities of cynicism or sadness, which are only undercurrents in the works.

1897

638.B Griffin, Montagu. "A Study of Thackeray." *Irish Monthly Magazine*, XXV (Jan.), 27-34; (Feb.), 66-75; (June), 290-302.
For T the novel was a parable rather than a study in psychology or manners. His continual irony would be intolerable were it not for his terseness. As a writer of burlesque T has

no equal. But only where he suppressed the satirist did his work become art.

639.A Crowe, Eyre. "Thackeray's Haunts and Homes." *Scribner's Magazine*, XXI (Jan.), 68-84; Rptd. as book (same title). New York: Scribner; London: Smith, Elder.
Descriptions and drawings of places frequented, lived in, and worked in by T.

640.B [Nicklin, J. A.]. "Thackeray's Philosophy." *Macmillan's Magazine*, LXXV (March), 343-347; Rptd. *Living Age*, CCXIII (May 1), 335-339.
The principal difference in estimates of T is in their attribution or denial of a philosophic note in his work. There is one, though it is not abstract or intellectual but moral: "Not to pitch one's standard too high . . . but to recognize, believe in, and cultivate . . . humility and kindness." At his worst T was merely satirical of inconsequential things. At his most serious, he was "the most trenchant adversary of the materialism . . . in the early years of the Victorian era." VF, P, and N are his truly representative works.

641.B Hunter, William W. *The Thackerays in India*. London: H. Frowde.
Chronicle of T's Anglo-Indian forebears, as well as a general family history and genealogy. "The greatest single influence of T's life-work was . . . his mother."

642.A James, Henry. *Harper's Weekly*, XLI (March 27), 315.
No. 641 above shows how much the British Empire was a heritage that helped shape T.

643.A Matthews, Brander. "My Favorite Novelist and His Best Book." *Munsey's Magazine*, XVII (May), 230-234; Rptd. *The Historical Novel and Other Essays*. New York: Scribner, 1901, pp. 147-162.
BL has been "shamefully neglected." In it the defects of serialization were "minimized or disappear altogether." Also T's inclination to the didactic—to moralizing—is almost completely eliminated. The method of narration is derived from *Castle Rackrent* ("with perhaps some memory of Fielding"), and the model for Barry is Casanova.

644.B Paul, Herbert. "The Apotheosis of the Novel Under Queen Victoria." *Nineteenth Century*, XLI (May), 769-792.
The prestige the novel now has was largely won by early Victorians such as Dickens, Thackeray, and C. Brontë. Education continually widens the circle of T's readers. Though T intruded himself in his novels, his consummate tact and style made him incapable of boring readers.

645.A Ogden, Rollo. "The New Pathos." *Atlantic Monthly*, LXXIX (June), 856-858; Rptd. *Current Literature*, XXIII (Jan. 1898), 15.
The effusive pathetic moods in fiction have given way to a more restrained rendering of sorrow (at least among first-rate writers). T, in this respect, anticipated the current fashion when he dealt with the deaths of George Osborne and Col. Newcome.

646.B Layard, George S. "On Some Caricature-Portraits of Thackeray By Pen and Pencil." *Good Words*, XXXVIII (Nov.), 702-708.
Some sketches are printed, others cited. Drawings are by Gavarni, Leech, and others.

647.A Brownell, William C. "William Makepeace Thackeray." *Library of the World's Best Literature.* Vol. XXXVI. New York: Peale & Hill, 14663-14672.
T's work is a "direct expression of his personality; and this personality is one of unusually special and conspicuous interest." The preacher and artist facets of him fuse in his work, producing an ideal combination for a novelist. The current charge that his view is sentimental rather than cynical is correct. T, like Fielding, is "social and moral," and though his world is less varied than Balzac's, it is more real. T's work does show the limitation resulting from dealing with externals, and even then with only "morally significant traits." But the method also has compensations: emphasis is placed on the importance of character, its complexity and deceptiveness; the full society—its manners and morals—is more fully examined. (See No. 674 below for a fuller statement of Brownell's ideas).

1898

648.BA Ritchie, Anne T. Biographical Introductions to *Works of William Makepeace Thackeray.* 13 vols. London: Smith, Elder, 1898-1899; New York: Harper, 1898-1899.
T's daughter presents information relating the works to the time in which they were written. Critical comment is at a minimum and primarily tries to reflect T's own opinions. T is quoted as saying: "VF is undoubtedly the best of my books." One can admire BL, but cannot like it. P is the "most cheerful" of the novels.

649.A G[ilder], J[eannette] L. "The New Thackeray." *Critic,* XXXII (April 16), 266-267.
Praise for No. 648 above and the new edition. T's own preference for VF supports the view of those who think it "one of the half-dozen great novels of the world."

650.B "The Reputation of Thackeray." *Academy,* LIII (April 30), 463-464.
VF, P, E, and N still hold their place and T's reputation not only survives but he becomes a classic. T has greater appeal today than for his own generation, in some respects, since his realism no longer offends. And it was he who was instrumental in this change of literary taste.

651.B *Athenaeum* (April 30), pp. 559-560.
T is being widely read. In contrast to notions of his cynicism, he is really as much a sentimentalist as Dickens. Though he was set against a biography, he revealed himself in his novels.

652.B *Spectator,* LXXX (April 30), 625-626.
VF (Biog. Ed.) is not merely a novel. "It is the book of society. It is a literature in itself." And it is to no purpose to criticize its obvious faults.

653.B "Thackeray's Foreigners." *Temple Bar,* CXIV (May), 83-92; Rptd. *Living Age,* CCXVII (June 25), 888-894.
Some non-English characters in the novels are listed, citing especially Paul de Florac (N) as perhaps the best example of T's fine understanding of a true Frenchman. Rarely are foreigners so well-developed in English fiction.

654.A G[ilder], J[eannette] L. "The Writing of *Pendennis*." *Critic*,
XXXII (May 28), 363-364.
It is impossible to see how P was ever called a work of caricature. "T said that his attempt was 'to tell the truth and to
tell it not unkindly,' and it seems . . . that he succeeded."

655.B *Literature*, II (July 2), 746-747.
In YP (Biog. Ed.) the beginnings of the development of T's
mastery can be traced. The introductions (No. 648 above),
though possessing a "silvery quality," would be more helpful
if the books were issued in the chronological order of original
publication.

656.A "Thackeray." New York *Times Saturday Review of Books
& Art* (July 2), p. 439.
The earliest stories and sketches (Biog. Ed., Vol. III) show
T's development. YP deserves higher distinction than most
of the other work.

657.A "Thackeray's *Barry Lyndon*." New York *Times Saturday Review of Books & Art* (July 23), pp. 481-482.
BL (Biog. Ed.) is "that one of all T's earlier works . . . which
seems worthiest of the author of VF and E."

658.A *Harper's Bazar*, XXXI (Aug. 6), 663.
BL (Biog. Ed.) shows how "T's masterly hand took as much
pain with a villain as with a saint, and both . . . have their
place [*sic*] in the . . . story of human life."

659.B [Lyall, Alfred C.]. "Thackeray." *Edinburgh Review*,
CLXXXVIII (Oct.), 378-409; Rptd. *Living Age*, CCXIX
(Dec. 24), 818-828; (Dec. 31), 883-895; *Studies in Litera-
ture and History*. London: Murray, 1915, pp. 76-120.
Review of *Works* (Biog. Ed.) deplores T's depiction of the
"dreary and ignoble side of English life" in earliest stories.
BL first showed "the promise and potency of T's genius." In
VF there is a "more indulgent irony" which continues to grow
in later work. But still "his descriptions of snobbery and
shams appear to us now overdrawn."

660.A "The Biographical Thackeray." New York *Times Saturday
Review of Books & Art* (Oct. 8), p. 660.

NEH (Biog. Ed.): "Parodies have lost much of their humorous charm, as all travesty will with age."

*661.A Sedgwick, Henry D. "Some Aspects of Thackeray." *Atlantic Monthly*, LXXXII (Nov.), 707-720; Rptd. *Essays on Great Writers*. Boston: Houghton-Mifflin, 1903, pp. 309-354.

T's work has a detrimental influence on society. He did not respond to the industrial revolution or concern himself with its problems. His proclaimed realism was no more than his following the "popular feeling" and reflecting its taste. P and N are merely sequels to VF in their meaning. Col. Newcome is made an "object of pity," and T never suggests that he should really be envied. This is because "T never departs from the British middle class conceptions of triumph and failure." Lacking "the poet's eye, he could not see and was not troubled." Satire is merely the weapon of a man at ease with himself, though at odds with the world; thus "satire is harmless as a moral weapon." "T was not a democrat," since he saw only men's differences rather than what they could share in common. "T was not a Christian. He acted upon all the standards which Christianity has proclaimed to be false." The man and the novelist must be judged as one; to distinguish the two is a heresy.

662.A "A Critic Assails Thackeray in the November *Atlantic*." New York *Times Saturday Review of Books & Art* (Nov. 12), p. 751.

No. 661 above elects to see only the grotesque and disagreeable. T, in contrast to that writer, is "truly Christian to the sinner in fiction," and in general shows surprising faith in all sorts of good people—especially women characters.

663.B "The Law and Lawyers of Thackeray." *Law Times*, CVI (Nov. 19), 59-60; Rptd. *Green Bag*, XI (Oct. 1899), 453-457.

T's brief legal career is mentioned, and then the scenes in P, AP, and S which show T's knowledge of the legal profession. "Most of his barrister heroes . . . are Bohemians and men about town first, and lawyers afterwards."

664.A *Harper's Bazar*, XXXI (Nov. 26), 1015-1016.
E (Biog. Ed.): "Certainly no finer English novel—none purer, more philosophical, and more dramatic—was ever written."

665.A Henry, Maria L. "A Word or Two About Thackeray's Women." New York *Times Saturday Review of Books & Art* (Nov. 26), p. 797.
Partially in response to No. 661 and No. 662 above: It is not T's bad women who are so objectionable, but rather his supposedly good women, who display such unlovely qualities. For example, Lady Castlewood's jealousy of her daughter, and Mrs. Pendennis' suspicions about Pen.

666.A "Two Neglected Women." New York *Times Saturday Review of Books & Art* (Nov. 26), p. 798.
T's portrayal of Caroline Brandon (SGS and AP) is commended, noting that he seems to have more affection for this character than for his well-known heroines.

667.B *Literature*, III (Dec. 3), 512-513.
E (Biog. Ed.) is T's most finished work from the artistic standpoint, largely because of his great effort on it and his familiarity and affection for that period of history.

668.A H., F. W. "Thackeray's Women." New York *Times Saturday Review of Books & Art* (Dec. 3), p. 812.
Reply to No. 665 above: "We are each and all stamped with the imperfections that characterize 'T's women.'"

669.A Henry, Maria L. "Thackeray's Women." New York *Times Saturday Review of Books & Art* (Dec. 17), p. 860.
Reply to No. 668 above: "The average woman may be capable of jealousy, the 'noble' woman is not." As typical of T's women, Mrs. Pendennis is not merely "unreasonable" but displays a "low mind" when she believes the anonymous note about her son.

670.A Droch. [pseud. of Robert Bridges]. *Life*, XXXII (Dec. 22), 526.
No. 648 above does not reveal a new T, but confirms "the old T who has grown so steadily into the first place in the hearts of lovers of English fiction." Because T didn't place

himself in a class apart from other people, he could write with truth and insight.

1899

†671.A Brown, Neal. "William Makepeace Thackeray." *Critical Confessions.* Wausau, Wisconsin: Privately printed, n.d., pp. 29-59.
T's work (more than that of other nineteenth-century authors) makes one feel warmth for the man behind the book. He deals with respectable wickedness in the main and his sermons are valuable since this wickedness is enticing. In spite of his worldly wisdom, he had "the heart of a child," and was "the historian, the epic poet of boyhood."

672.A *Bookman* (New York), VIII (Jan.), 420-422.
No. 661 above "assumes a moral vantage to which it has no right." T was not a passionate reformer, nor was his world a fairyland; but these are no grounds for condemnation. No. 661 obviously does not want men and women in fiction, "but stained glass figures that teach something or preach something."

673.A Droch. [pseud. of Robert Bridges]. *Life,* XXXIII (Jan. 12), 26.
Information in Vol. IX of No. 648 above shows that T's complaints about writing were "as though the developed conscience of the rare artist were forever goading him on and spoiling the fun he ought to have had out of the exercise of his fancy."

*674.A Brownell, William C. "William Makepeace Thackeray." *Scribner's Magazine,* XXV (Feb.), 236-249; Rptd. *Victorian Prose Masters.* New York: Scribner, 1901, pp. 1-46.
A narrow view of the aesthetics of the novel can only "circumscribe its area of interest and limit its range of expression." The presence of an author in his work does not necessarily destroy aesthetic form. The true criterion is the sense of life that is finally imparted. T intrudes himself on his scene, but with the result of enhancing rather than restricting its reality, of deepening rather than destroying its illusion. His "technic" is not that of a miniaturist, but of one who

never loses sight of large scale relations and atmosphere. Compared to James's "filling life around character," T's method is a "short-cut to verisimilitude . . . with more color, more personal feeling . . . attuning the reader to the rhythm of the subject" and establishing a relationship between things. His talk is not there to "round out" characters, but presumes their independent existence. The problem is that when personal expression is as easy and as successful as it is for T, it can be overused. T had no talent for abstract thought, and thus his philosophy is moral rather than metaphysical, revolving around the importance of "character"—its complexity and deceptiveness. His concentration on elemental and morally significant traits permits a concurrent analysis of the society itself. However, for T, "character is spectacle . . . and not the illustrative incarnation of interesting traits and tendencies." It is distinctively literary rather than scientific. T's style is that of a great writer, even for those who otherwise find serious fault with his work. "His language produces the effect of richness by its fullness rather than by scrupulous selection of epithet."

675.A Parsons, Florence M. "After Reading Thackeray." *Literature* (New York), N.S. I (Feb. 10), 99-100.
The quality of cynicism was unjustly ascribed to T, who actually was "the first pessimist, save Swift, in English prose fiction." His kind of pessimism is "never grim" and it constitutes his appeal. In large measure it has taken hold, so that now it seems to be the general atmosphere.

*676.B Layard, George S. "Our Graphic Humourists: W. M. Thackeray." *Magazine of Art*, XXIII (April), 256-262.
T's limited skill as a graphic artist forced him to put all his subtle humor into writing. Nevertheless his bad drawings do convey much of value. The principal quality of his many sketches, like that of his poems, is their unrestraint.

677.A Cross, Wilbur L. "The Return to Realism." *The Development of the English Novel*. New York: Macmillan, pp. 196-211 and *passim*.
"T was a critic of rare insight," and promoted the mood of realism in such work as NEH as well as VF. However, his moral viewpoint was that of an eighteenth-century essayist, and to appreciate VF fully we must grant T "the reactionary

mood and the satirical license." VF should also be considered in the light of the picaresque tradition. It and N are both "epic in their immense scope" and are "more rigidly dramatic" than their apparent carelessness would indicate. Essentially T was a comic writer, but with "a literary sentimentalism," like Sterne's, mixed in, thus producing his humor (p. 259).

678.B Melville, Lewis. [pseud. of Lewis S. Benjamin]. *The Life of William Makepeace Thackeray.* 2 vols. London: Hutchinson.
(A non-definitive biography, using all published materials though no private documents.) Sympathetic study of T's work and life reveals "the sensitive man" who "had covered his real self." Though he was no cynic, the theme of *vanitas* is at the heart of his philosophy, and "the sadness that pervaded his life tinged his writings." T's genius first shone through in BL. (No extensive critical comments are offered though the opinions of other critics are presented throughout.)

679.B *Times*, Sept. 27, p. 9.
No. 678 above is neither critical work nor biography. A man of T's powers and reputation deserves better.

680.B *Athenaeum* (Oct. 7), p. 491.
No. 678 above is merely a "collection of scraps . . . totally unworthy of its subject."

681.A "Thackeray." New York *Times Saturday Review of Books & Art* (Oct. 14), pp. 689-690.
No. 678 above is a "mere undigested mass of facts" that are "badly arranged," and add little to our knowledge of "one of the greatest, if not the greatest, name in the century's literary history."

682.B "The Husk of a Novelist." *Academy*, LVII (Oct. 21), 447-448.
No. 678 above is hampered by lack of private documents and even an industrious collecton of published material cannot reveal T's inner personality, which is the thing of real importance.

683.A "Thackeray the Cynic Indeed." New York *Times Saturday Review of Books & Art* (Oct. 21), p. 712.

The facts of T's life (the testimony of his friends) and the "texts T constantly preached" make the charge of cynicism "entirely unwarrantable."

684.B *Saturday Review*, LXXXVIII (Oct. 28), 554-555.

No. 678 above is "all that scissors and paste can achieve," but not a real biography, which might give sense to one who "was both a great man and a great writer," and at the same time both "a child and a giant."

685.A M[aurice], A[rthur] B. "Thackeray's Becky." *Bookman* (New York), X (Nov.), 239-244.

VF was the book that taught T how to write as well as shaping all of his moral force. Becky was never a source of aversion to T; but, "committed to the task of making her odious, [he] began and maintained an attack which was unjust." Thus she has been interpreted "as a supreme type of hypocrisy," of which trait she is completely free. However, T was also dazzled by Becky's triumphs and at her apogee we can "suspect that T lost control of his creation" and forgot to make her odious.

686.B *Spectator*, LXXXIII (Nov. 18), 733.

No. 678 above is "the inept laudation of an incompetent judge," though useful for the bibliography.

1900

687.B [Sichel, E. H.]. "The Sentiment of Thackeray." *Quarterly Review*, CXCI (Jan.), 138-153; Rptd. *Living Age*, CCXXIV (March 24), 745-756; *Eclectic Magazine*, CXXXIV (May), 619-630.

"Reverence, humility, charity were the watchwords of T's creed—the only dogmas he inculcated. . . . A kind of loving good sense is characteristic of all T's religion." He was a subjective writer and liked to display a true sentiment. Thus, though called a realist for opposing the school of high-flown romance, he is not much like the realists of today. No. 678 above fails to give a "living picture." No. 648 above shows warmth and "style."

688.A "A Life of Thackeray." *Independent*, LII (Jan. 4), 65-66.
No. 678 above provides "at last . . . a good and full biography." "T was on odd man, so odd that he stands among great writers as a play of nature. He fell into autobiography whenever he talked or wrote. . . . T the man and T the novelist were identical." T's levity is such that "he somehow seems too much a jester."

689.A Frank, Maude. "Thackeray—A Protest." *Book Buyer*, XX (Feb.), 22-24.
Young people are encouraged to read VF and its popularity is very great among collegians. But perhaps it would be better for them to prefer the "latest piece of affectation to the masterpiece which must teach them lessons of doubt and disillusion." To see how a brother and sister will not remain friends through life is but one of VF's "cruel truths."

690.A Dickson, Frederick S. *Book Buyer*, XX (March), 99-100.
No. 689 above does not suggest that T's conclusions are false, but that they are "cruel truths." "Can any truth be . . . *as* cruel as the lie which would hide it?"

691.A Maurice, Arthur B. "Some Thackerayan Ideas About Americans." *Bookman* (New York), XI (March), 59-61.
Neither T nor Dickens liked America despite the fact that each had warm personal friendships there. They did not have real sympathy with the spirit of the people. This was more excusable for T, who also was "quite as unjust and narrow in his estimate of the French." Characterizations in SFN, PSB, and P (the cook Alcide) are examples of his attitude.

[692.]A Gerwig, George W. "*Henry Esmond* and *Richard Carvel*." *Criterion*; as reported in *Current Literature*, XXVII (March), 211.
The title books are compared, showing "the progress which has been made in the art of writing." In *Carvel* the interest is immediate, whereas in E the "one superb dramatic situation . . . which might have been told . . . in 20,000 words is dragged out to 200,000."

693.B "William Makepeace Thackeray." *Church Quarterly Review*, L (April), 78-91.
The novel is again becoming objectionable. The good tradi-

tion of Austen and Scott had been kept up by writers like T. No. 678 above is poor work, but "anything the public can learn about a man like T is . . . clear gain." T revolted from Puritanism, not orthodoxy. His truly reverent spirit kept him from writing on improper subjects. Essentially all his portraits of clergymen are true ones. The two key secrets of T's life are religion and early disappointment.

*694.A Merrill, Katharine. "Characterization in the Beginning of Thackeray's *Pendennis.*" *PMLA*, XV (June), 233-252.

The first 200 odd pages of P reveal that "T inclines to use the more internal and direct means of portrayal" rather than the "external modes . . . , i.e., comment or description." His ability to present characters vividly and almost completely even in a single scene "lies in the simplicity of character and in the predominant use of the dramatic method." In addition, "his habit of minute observation" (though sometimes tending to "lengthiness or even dullness") at its best records detailed gestures that create an "effect . . . like that of a theatrical performance."

695.A Sherwood, Mary E. W. "Heroines." New York *Times Saturday Review of Books & Art* (Sept. 15), p. 612.

"Excepting . . . dear Ethel Newcome, the most delightful girl who ever lived," T's heroines are unlikeable. Laura (P) with her gardening shears was "too terribly square and self-conscious." Becky is not a true heroine, "except as Jezabel [*sic*] and Athalia are heroines." Nor is VF really a novel (though it is a satire), because "the mission of the novelist . . . is next to that of the royal Psalmist—to comfort us in our affliction."

696.A Payne, Leonidas W. "Thackeray." *Sewanee Review*, VIII (Oct.), 437-456.

No. 678 above is a collection of old material, but because of its bibliography it is a "fairly good reference book." T was not a cynic personally, though, "with the exception of E, all of T's novels may be placed under the general title of VF." No novelist "talked face to face with the reader so persistently and so personally." Thus "we are drawn to the personality of the man." The key to T's source of power in his work is "sympathy."

*697.A Howells, William D. "Thackeray's Bad Heroines." *Harper's Bazar*, XXXIII (Nov. 17), 1799-1804; Rptd. *Heroines of Fiction*. 2 vols. New York: Harper, 1901, I, 190-202.

In spite of T being a realist in inclination, "he talked of fiction as a fable-land, when he ought to have known it and proclaimed it as the very home of truth." Nevertheless, he was a great talent "and the Ever-Womanly revealed herself to him as she had not to any other English novelist since Jane Austen's time." "T's bad heroines are truer than his good ones." The best of them is Becky, beside whom Beatrix (E) is thin and factitious, and Blanche (N) becomes a literary affectation. T's "art is quite unerring in result, though it is mostly . . . so bad in process."

*698.A Howells, William D. "Thackeray's Good Heroines." *Harper's Bazar*, XXXIII (Dec. 1), 1945-1950; Rptd. *Heroines of Fiction*. 2 vols. New York: Harper, 1901, I, 203-214.

Just as T found good in bad heroines, he was also "the discoverer . . . of the fallibility of angels; but he had not the courage of his facts." He tried to offset the defects by overdoing the virtues. The love of Esmond and Rachel seems to be an afterthought rather than something in strict keeping with "the line of probability," and thus it creates the "unhandsome dénouement," which "does not seem either nice or true." P is T's "supreme effort in respect to its women, the ultimate test of greatness in a novel."

*699.A Howells, William D. "Thackeray's Ethel Newcome and Charlotte Brontë's Jane Eyre." *Harper's Bazar*, XXXIII (Dec. 15), 2094-2100; Rptd. *Heroines of Fiction*. 2 vols. New York: Harper, 1901, I, 215-227.

Ethel is T's best effort at "a character of noble but not unnatural beauty." He succeeds admirably in making us feel her growth. "Ethel sums up . . . the virtues and defects of the highest type of T women, and as women go the type is not so low as might be, though he used to be accused of such a cynical hatred of women." However, "no heroine of T's except Becky Sharp seems . . . quite so alive as . . . Jane Eyre."

700.B Gwynn, Stephen. Introduction to *Pendennis*. 3 vols. London: Methuen, I, ix-xxxvi.

In P, T did not have a story to tell from the start as he had in VF and E, merely a theme to develop. Nor does it have the "intellectual or emotional pitch of its predecessor." But it contains "the finest study of calf-love ever drawn," and its picture of literary Bohemia "surpasses Murger . . . in force and intensity."

1901

701.B Monson, Edward. "Thackeray's Women." *Gentleman's Magazine*, CCXC (Jan.), 30-35.
T's ideal woman is "the hearth and home being." Despite his frequent depiction of women as either weak or wicked, T basically tried to show how really hard their lives were. T's "knight errant" sentiments will outlive the current fashions of "smart society" or the "wild women." "Laura is T's most satisfactory specimen of womankind."

702.A James, Henry. "Winchelsea, Rye and *Denis Duval*." *Scribner's Magazine*, XXIX (Jan.), 44-53.
The influence and relation of the two named towns with DD can be seen. Various surmises are possible regarding T's intentions for the book but none of T's hints or the scenes themselves give an idea that DD would have been anything more than adventure—a "picturesque affair."

*703.B "One Aspect of Thackeray." *Temple Bar*, CXXIV (Sept.), 73-78.
T's works interweave many of the same characters, and, what is more, he develops the family connections between many others—emphasizing family traits no less than individual tendencies. T rarely makes a slip in these complicated, though not overly obvious, genealogies.

704.A Whiteley, Emily S. "*Esmond* and *Les Rois en Exile*." *Critic*, XXXIX (Oct.), 368-369.
A comparison of the two novels shows that both T's pretender in E and Daudet's king share a mocking wit and a lack of discretion. But, whereas the Queen of Illyria is a simple character, Lady Castlewood is one of the most complex T ever created. Her contradictions and surprises tend to "place her among the living." Both women, however, show similar attitudes towards love.

705.A Wilson, James G. "Thackeray in the United States," *Century*, LXIII (Dec.), 221-237; (Jan. 1902), 335-354; Rptd. *Cornhill*, N.S. XI (Dec.), 721-741; N.S. XII (Jan. 1902), 1-26; information incorporated in book (same title), New York: Dodd, Mead, 1904; London: Smith, Elder, 1904. An account of T's two visits to the U.S. (1852-1853 and 1855-1856).

INDEX

Index

This index covers material both from the introductory text and from the bibliography itself. References to the introduction are indicated by *page number* in *italic type* and precede other references under the same heading and modification. References to items in the bibliography are indicated by their entry numbers and are printed in roman type. An asterisk before an entry number indicates an item of particular critical and/or historical interest. One abbreviation is used in this index: T for Thackeray.

The categories of critical topics and concerns relevant to Thackeray and to Victorian fiction in general are correlated in order to suggest connections and conclusions not explicitly developed elsewhere in this book.

A

Addison, Joseph, T's view of, 163, 164, 166, 167, 271, 274; T like, 206
Adventures of Philip, The. See *Philip*
Ainsworth, William H., 216
Alison, Archibald, 250
Anderson, R. H., 430
Art critic, T as, 405, *474, 570, 600, 678
Art of fiction. *See* Fiction
Austen, Jane, and T compared, *54, *275, *474, 548

B

B., H., 510
B., H. R., 528
Bagehot, Walter, 437, 486
Ballads. See Poetry
Balzac, Honoré de, T compared with, 407, 496, *549, 630, 647; T's opinion of, 566
Barnes, James N., 508
Barry Lyndon, 6, 25, 247, 252, 258, *275, 360, 375, 386, *474, *484, 508, *520, *539, *549, 557, 558, 575, 603, *624, 626, 632, 633, 643, 648, 657-659, 678
Bayne, Alicia, 538
Bayne, Peter, 387
Bedingfield, Richard, 515
Bell, Robert, 9; criticism by, *75
Benjamin, Lewis S., 678
Bennett, James Gordon, 192, 223, 334
Berdmore, Septimus, 495
Bibb, Grace C., 537
Biographies of T. *See* Thackeray, biographical accounts
Blanchard, Laman, 21

*507, *549, 617, 630, 696; moral function of, 65, 68, *89, 112, 186, *201, 370, 488, 534, 561, *661, 677; satirist contra novelist (artist), 68, *73, 138, 146, *151, 250, *423, *474, *554, *572, 603, 605, 606, 638, 695; and humor, 405, 456, *459, *482, *507, 603, 606, 630; result of T's sensibility, 486, 487. *See also* Mean aspects of life; Moral instruction, as element of fiction; Sentiment(ality), mixed with satire

Scott, Sir Walter, T like, 210, 218, 410, 467, 518; and T compared, *474, 612

Second Funeral of Napoleon, The, 13-17, 405, *624, 648, 678, 691

Sedgwick, Arthur G., 545

Sedgwick, Henry D., *22*; criticism by, *661

Senior, Nassau W., 300

Sentiment(ality) in T's work, *16*, 25, 70, *149, 316, 319, 388, 428, 456, 628, 645, 647, 651, *674, 677, 687, 701; mixed with humor, 21, 23, 28, 45, 332, 362; lack of, 32, 64, 68, *73, 79, 141, 142, 188, 204, 216, 217, 325, 328, 447, *451, 462, 563; mixed with satire, *75, 83, 96, 112, 185, 246, 365, 409, 415, *459. *See also* Humor; Satire, gentleness of

Serialization of fiction, effects of, 18, *72, *73, 79, 104, 130, 132, *139, *148, *149, 154, *221, 296, *357, 408, 410, 508, 643. *See also* Fiction, aesthetics of

Shabby Genteel Story, A, 239, *474, *624, 648, 678

Shakespeare, William, T like, 203, 327, 430, *474, 495, 613

Shearer, Sextus, 417

Sherwood, Mary E. W., 695

Sichel, E. H., 687

Sichel, Walter, 587

Simms, William G., 146, 196, 366, 413

Simpson, Richard, *19*; criticism by, *485

Skepticism, reflected in T's work, 359, *368, *482, 521. *See also* Cynicism; Mean aspects of life, betrays

faulty morality; Melancholy view of life; Philosophy of T

Smith, George B., 523

Smith, Goldwin, 404

Smollett, Tobias G., T like, 3, 261; T's view of, 229

Snobbery of T revealed in work, *22*, *554, 592; anti-, *148, 150, 308, *555, *626. *See also Book of Snobs*; Gentlemanly interest; Thackeray, imputed snobbery

Social class, gentleman's. *See* Gentlemanly interest

Social milieu, as focus of T's work, *26*, 203, 318, 392, *507, 647, 652, *674, 677. *See also* Satire, moral function of

Steele, Richard, T's view of, 170, 173, 274, 506; T like, 487

Stephen, James Fitzjames, *6*, *30*, *33n*; criticism by, 375, *484

Stephen, Leslie, *20-21*; criticism by, *549

Sterne, Laurence, T's view of, 181, 182, 231, 271, 274, 486, 512, 563; T like, 486, 677; T contrasted with, 563

Stevenson, Robert Louis, *22*; criticism by, 592

Stoddard, Richard H., 525, 527

Stowe, Harriet Beecher, *Uncle Tom's Cabin* contra T's work, 304

Strong, George T., *8*

Stubbs's Calendar, published in U.S.A,. *5*; criticism of, 126, 127

Sturgis, Russell, 553

Style of T's writing, in *Esmond*, *12*, 198, 200, 204, 206, 212, 214, *221, 237; authorial intrusion, *18*, 25, *29-30*, 106, 204, 206, 214, *275, 300, 315, 402, 434, 439, 445, 510, 516, 526, 603, 606, 638, 644, *674, 677, *697; colloquial quality, *26-27*, 41, 63, 161, *357, 593, 677, 696; general characteristics, 8, 48, *54, 57, 60, 68, *73, 79, 120, 131, *134, *148, *151, 220, 274, 287, 295, 320, *321, *368, 403, 408, 410, 445, 450, 491, *507, 526, 568, 569, 590, 619, *624, 647, *674, 678; mixture of styles, *17, 24, 33, 200, 280, 312. *See also* Fiction, T's pan-